Dogs

Dogs

CONSULTANT EDITOR
Paul McGreevy
B.VSc. Ph.D. M.R.C.V.S.

FOG CITY PRESS

Published by Fog City Press
814 Montgomery Street
San Francisco, CA 94133 USA

Chief Executive Officer John Owen
President Terry Newell
Publisher Lynn Humphries
Managing Editor Janine Flew
Art Director Kylie Mulquin
Editorial Coordinator Tracey Gibson
Editorial Assistants Marney Richardson, Kiren Thandi
Production Manager Martha Malic-Chavez
Business Manager Emily Jahn
Vice President International Sales Stuart Laurence
European Sales Director Vanessa Mori

Project Editor Lynn Cole
Designer Katie Ravich
Consultant Editor Dr Paul McGreevy B.V.Sc. Ph.D. M.R.C.V.S.

ISBN 1 876778 77 6

Color reproduction by Colourscan Co Pte Ltd
Printed by LeeFung-Asco Printers
Printed in China

A Weldon Owen Production

Welcome to the
Home Reference Library

We have created this exciting new series of books with the help of an international team of consultants, writers, editors, photographers, and illustrators, all of whom share our common vision—the desire to convey our passion and enthusiasm for the natural world through books that are enjoyable to read, authoritative as a source of reference, and fun to collect.

Finding out about things *should* be fun. That's the basic premise of the *Home Reference Library*. So, we've ensured that every picture tells a story, every caption encapsulates a fascinating fact, and every paragraph contains useful or interesting information.

It is said that seeing is believing. We believe seeing is understanding, too. That's why in the *Home Reference Library* we have combined text and images in an imaginative, dynamic design style that conveys the excitement of finding out about the natural world. Cut-away cross-sections detail the inner workings of a termite mound or the 2,000-million-year-old rock strata of the Grand Canyon. Photographs reveal extraordinary facts about the minutest forms of animal life, aspects of the behavior of nature's fiercest predators, or the beauty of a world far beyond our planet.

Each handy-sized book is a complete source of reference on its subject. Collect all the titles in the *Home Reference Library* series to compile an invaluable encyclopedic resource that you'll return to again and again.

From the editors of the *Home Reference Library.*

An agreeable companion on a journey
is as good as a carriage.

Moral Sayings,
Publilius Syrus (1st century BC), Roman philosopher

CONTENTS

THE DOG IN YOUR LIFE

There is something special about the unconditional devotion dogs lavish upon their owners.

Choosing Your Dog

THE RELATIONSHIP BETWEEN A PERSON and a dog can be one
of life's most rewarding experiences. To give this
relationship the best chance of success, choose your pet
carefully. Consider your lifestyle, your home environment
and your family needs. Too often, a dog is chosen with
little forethought and does not live up to an owner's
expectations—with heartbreaking consequences.
The key to a successful relationship between you and
your pet is to make the right choice in the first place.

CHOOSING THE RIGHT DOG

Before taking on the responsibility of a dog, make sure that the whole family is willing to care for him. Feeding, play, exercise, grooming and training are all essential canine needs and most involve time and expense. If there are enough committed caretakers, your next step is to decide exactly what kind of dog you want.

WHICH BREED?

Although individuals vary from dog to dog, breeds tend to have predictable character traits and appearance. Learn as much as you can about the characteristics of different breeds so you can narrow your choices.

Don't forget that breeding of genetically similar dogs can result in diseases, such as hip dysplasia, and behavioral problems, such as aggression. Mixed breeds often make excellent pets and adopting one is a good way to avoid inherited diseases.

A MATTER OF CHOICE Luckily, dogs come in so many sizes, colors and shapes, as this Golden Retriever and Corgi demonstrate, that there's one to suit all tastes.

Time and space Don't choose a very active dog unless you have the time and space to give it the exercise it needs. Bored dogs tend to become destructive. For apartment dwellers, less active breeds may be best. Toy breeds can get plenty of exercise right in the hall of your apartment (but some are quite noisy). Despite their size, giant breeds, like Newfoundlands and Great Danes, tend to be sedate and need little exercise.

Coat length Think about the grooming requirements of your dog. Long-coated dogs, such as Chow Chows and Keeshonds, have beautiful thick coats but it takes a good deal of time and effort to keep them that way. Short-coated dogs, such as Labradors and Dalmatians, take less grooming but tend to shed hair all year round. Breeds that don't shed, such as Poodles and Bichon Frises, must be clipped regularly, which is an additional expense if done professionally.

Male or female In general, males may be more inclined to fight and have more behavioral problems

DROOLING BREEDS

Like this Golden Retriever, all breeds drool when there's food around. But when it comes to too much saliva in all the wrong places, Saint Bernards, Newfoundlands and Basset Hounds are the worst offenders. It's because their lips can't hold back the flood.

than females, so families with children may be better with a female as a first-time pet. Dogs of either sex are equally good as companions or watchdogs.

Consider cost Before you take the final step, think about the cost of food, leashes, toys and veterinary care, not to mention replacement of demolished household items. You may also need to build a fence or hire a dog-walker.

PUPPY OR OLDER DOG?

While puppies have obvious appeal, chewed shoes, housetraining and the other rigors of puppyhood are not for every family. Some people will wisely choose to adopt an older dog.

A DOG THAT NEEDS A HOME

Don't adopt a dog, whether from a shelter or another family, just because you feel sorry for it. Although many adult dogs up for adoption make wonderful pets, some have behavioral problems that might not be obvious. Try to obtain an accurate history of the animal. If you choose carefully, an adult dog may be perfect for you. Also, you'll have adopted an animal that really needs a home.

WHAT ABOUT A PUPPY?

If you get a puppy, you will have more control over his learning during the crucial first few months of life. If you have children, your puppy will grow up with them, learning to be tolerant and unafraid of children in general. Try to get your new puppy between six and eight weeks of age. It's important for the development of social behavior that a pup stays with her mother and littermates until this time. However, as a six- to eight-week-old puppy is in the midst of the "period of socialization"

MEET THE FAMILY This Weimaraner pup will soon be as big as its father. Ask to see both the puppy's parents, if possible.

(between three weeks and three months of age), it's just as important that your new pup starts to bond you with now.

Once you have decided which breed, find a reliable breeder—your vet, local breed club or national kennel club should be able to help you with this. Choose your puppy from a healthy litter. Make sure all the puppies appear bright, alert, active and well-fed. Play with them and pick up each one individually. Try to avoid the most bossy or most shy puppies in the litter. If possible, arrange to meet the puppy's parents and other adult relatives.

HERE ARE SOME THINGS TO WATCH FOR Reputable breeders make tremendous efforts to ensure that the dogs they sell are healthy and not prone to long-term problems, but you can improve your chances by checking for certain signs.

Eyes Clear, bright and shiny, not bloodshot; free of discharge or watering. Eyelashes should not touch the eyeball.

Nose Usually cold and wet but not running.

Ears Clean, free of odor, discharge or excess wax.

Coat Glossy and clean, with no fleas, dandruff or excess oil. It will feel shorter and thinner than an adult's.

Mouth Gums should be firm, either pink or pigmented. Breath should smell clean.

Skin When the hair is parted, skin is smooth, free of parasites, lumps and sores. The color will range from pink to black, depending on the breed.

Movement Puppy should move freely, favoring no individual paw or leg.

DOGS AND CHILDREN

If you and your family don't have a dog, then chances are your children haven't had much exposure to dogs. That means they won't have much idea about what dogs do and don't like. They might also be a bit tentative and nervous around this hairy thing that pants and barks and seems almost as big as they are. Your children will need to be well prepared for the arrival of your new family member, so that they can be confident and careful dog lovers. Give them opportunities to meet other people's dogs or, better still, their puppies.

GETTING TO KNOW EACH OTHER
Children must learn how to behave around a dog, and how to handle one properly, particularly if it's a pup. A dog is not a toy. Children must be gentle, and not too rowdy to begin with, until your dog is used to them. Always make sure there's an adult around to supervise when children are playing with your new dog. You will then be assured of everyone's safety and enjoyment until you are confident that they are all consistently doing the right thing.

Find a training school for your dog that will let children take part or, if they are too young, at least where they'll be allowed to watch.

Rough games Explain to your children that when they play rough, the puppy can lose control and may bite in its eagerness to join in the fun. If this happens, tell them to squeal like another puppy, even if the nip didn't hurt much. This is how puppies learn not to bite one another. Encourage

GOOD MANNERS This Golden Retriever is learning to beg politely. Everyone in the family can help to train your dog. Just see that they all go about it in the same way.

your children to play quiet games with the puppy until everyone understands the rules.

SUITABLE BREEDS

These friendly and playful breeds are good with young children:

- Bearded Collie
- Boxer
- Golden or Flat-coated Retrievers
- Labrador Retriever
- Miniature Schnauzer
- Shetland Sheepdog
- Standard Poodle
- Yorkshire Terrier

TAKING RESPONSIBILITY Don't buy a dog for a child on the condition that the child alone must take care of it. A dog will not teach your child responsibility; you must be willing to see that the dog is properly cared for at all times.

BE AWARE

Children under three may be unintentionally rough with their pets. Dogs, too, can be rough with very young children. Even those breeds listed at left require consistent training and positive early experiences with children to be fully reliable.

Living with Your Dog

YOUR NEW DOG WILL BRING you many years of love,
fun, companionship and happiness. You can get your
relationship off to a good start and make the adjustment
easier for both of you by preparing in advance for the
changes you will need to make in your home.

YOUR NEW PET

Before your new pup arrives, think about his basic needs. Where will he sleep? How will you take him out for exercise? What will he play with?

BEDDING

The first thing your new dog needs is a comfortable bed in a place of his own. For a puppy, a box turned on its side and lined with soft, washable bedding, or a chew-proof pad inside a pen is perfect. For an adult dog, a durable dog bed (the bean bag type) or soft blanket would be greatly appreciated. Find a quiet, warm area away from drafts but close to the family. Young pups sleep for up to 20 hours a day!

A traveling box or crate Buy one that will be large enough for your puppy when he is fully grown.

COLLARS AND LEASHES

Flat collars are best for a puppy because they can be adjusted as he grows. Choose one made of nylon or leather, which he can wear at all times. As puppies tend to chew, nylon leashes are best. Leather or nylon collars and leashes are also ideal for mature dogs. When you fit your dog's collar, it should be loose enough to be comfortable but not so loose that he will be able to slip out of it. You should be able to fit two fingers under a collar that's the right size. Other types of collars are used for training and for dogs who pull when on a leash. Choke chains are not recommended.

An extendable leash is another useful accessory. Usually made with a comfortable plastic handle, it will give your dog freedom to explore, but allow him to be easily reeled in when necessary.

THE HALTI COLLAR allows you to guide your dog's head around to the direction you want to go without hurting him.

THE NEW ARRIVAL Give some thought beforehand to the accommodation and belongings your new dog will need. Good planning will make it much easier for him to adjust to his new surroundings.

OTHER ACCESSORIES

While you are at the pet supply store, pick up some safe chew toys, a soft bristle brush and cleaning solution for the inevitable accidents that even mature dogs may have while adjusting to a new home.

ABSOLUTELY ESSENTIAL Your dog should have a microchip, but also attach an identity tag to his collar. This should be inscribed with your name, address and phone number and worn at all times.

DOG-PROOFING YOUR HOME

The first thing your new dog will do is check out her new surroundings. Dog-proofing your home is a lot like child-proofing—it basically means removing anything that may be a danger to the dog or anything that is at risk of being broken. To prevent electric shocks or a bump on the head from a heavy appliance, unplug electrical cords or secure them out of reach. A dangling cord is an irresistible temptation to a young pup.

Keep all cleaning compounds, solvents and other dangerous materials in a secure place. Insect sprays, snail, slug and rodent poisons, and antifreeze can all be poisonous if ingested by a dog. Finally, remove breakable objects that have sentimental value.

NATURAL CURIOSITY The things your dog will gulp down if she gets the chance will astonish you. Don't risk her safety; store cleaning products in lockable cupboards.

KEEP OUT OF REACH Something in his owner's purse has caught the attention of this Hungarian Vizsla. Items such as chocolate and medications pose a serious risk to your pet.

CHEWING

When puppies are between three and six months of age, their new teeth begin to emerge, causing them pain. Chewing on a hard object may relieve some of this discomfort, so get some "chew" toys that will satisfy your dog's need to chew. They will also help exercise her jaws and clean her teeth. A variety of nylon bones, rope bones, rawhides, fleece toys and "sterilized" real bones will keep your dog busy for hours. Buy new ones or rotate the old ones every week so that they remain more interesting than your shoes or the legs of the kitchen table.

TOYS

Your dog can't tell the difference between your children's toys and those you provide for her to chew, so it's best to keep doors to bedrooms and children's play areas closed. Two other hazards found in adult bedrooms are nylon stockings and medications of various kinds. Stockings are easily swallowed and can obstruct your dog's intestines, while an overdose of a human medication is as big a threat to her as it is to a small child. Jewelry and small change may also attract her to do a taste test.

A selection of chew toys

DOG-PROOFING YOUR YARD

If you have a yard, check the fencing to see that it is secure enough to keep a dog inside. If there are any holes, fix them. For a small dog, a fence that is 4 feet (1.2 m) high should be adequate, while a 6-foot (1.8 m) fence will hold most large dogs. Bear in mind that some dogs, such as terriers, are diggers by nature and will dig under a fence if it is not fully secured. Make sure that the gate shuts firmly and that a small dog would be unable to squeeze itself underneath it. Swimming pools or ponds should also be covered or fenced.

An alternative to a fenced yard is an enclosed, outdoor pen. If you are planning to erect one, make it large enough for a good game of fetch. Also, if you plan to keep your dog in the pen for several hours at a time, provide a dog house for shelter from the elements. If you have a large working dog, such as a Mastiff or a Great Dane, he might be more comfortable outside in a kennel than inside the house.

OPEN AND SHUT
A well-designed dog door can be locked, if necessary, but otherwise allows your dog, like this American Bulldog, to go in and out at will.

POISONOUS PLANTS

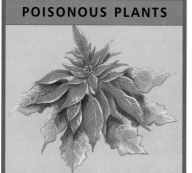

The following house and garden plants can be toxic to dogs if eaten in sufficient quantities: poinsettia (leaves), azaleas and rhododendrons (green leaves), dumb cane (leaves), Japanese yew (needles, bark, seed), oleander (leaves, stems, bark), English ivy (fruit), mushroom (*Amanita* species), precatory bean (seeds) and castor bean (seeds).

Your dog's kennel should be sufficiently large for him to move around freely inside. Consult a local expert for advice about a suitable kennel design. The first few times you let your new dog out into your yard or kennel, do not leave him alone. Dogs can be Houdinis if left unattended.

EXTRA PRECAUTIONS

Provide shelter from rain and sun and, if your dog must be tied up, make sure that the rope or chain can't become tangled. Remove choke collars and dangling tags that could become snagged.

IRRESISTIBLE It doesn't mean that you dog is hungry if, like this Labrador mix, he can't resist the trash. You must simply protect him from the temptation.

Getting Settled In

SAFE PLACE Your puppy should regard her crate as a safe place where she plays and eats—never as a place of punishment.

When you first bring your new puppy or dog home, she will probably be somewhat confused and apprehensive. Once indoors, restrict your pup to one room. Let her sniff around and familiarize herself with her surroundings. Introduce her to her bed and food and water bowls. Be gentle with her. Praise her for little things, such as being bold, playful and beautiful. Don't speak harshly or punish your new dog. She must learn to trust, not fear you during these first few days. You'll have plenty of time to train her after the adjustment period.

Try not to have friends around to the house until your new pet has settled in. Let her get used to you and your family first, before introducing her to strangers. Teach your children to be gentle and quiet around the new dog, especially if she's a puppy. Children must learn that puppies are not toys and need to be left alone when resting or eating.

Meeting other pets

Introductions to the household's established pets should be made gradually and under constant supervision. Many older dogs and cats resent the arrival of a puppy, so don't leave them alone together at first, unless the puppy is in a protected pen. Let the established pets sniff the newcomer through the pen. Always give your older animals the most attention; never let them feel that they are being replaced. Also, to prevent "food wars," feed the animals separately until they are quite comfortable with each other.

Meeting your other dog It's best if the two dogs meet in neutral territory, say at the park. When the two dogs are together at home, put the new dog in its indoor kennel or crate until the two start to make friends.

Meeting your cat Hold your new dog tightly, not the cat. The cat will probably fluff itself up, hiss, spit and run away. Don't let the dog chase the cat. Try to get the dog's attention away from the cat by shaking a noisy toy. Repeat the meetings until the two get used to each other.

MEETING THE FAMILY Let the new dog make the approaches to each person as she feels inclined. Don't rush her. Kneel down and let her sniff your hand until she is at ease with more touching.

When You Go Away

Before deciding whether or not to take your dog on vacation with you, consider the condition of the dog, your mode of travel and the nature of the destination. Dogs who get nervous or carsick when they travel, those who are sick or aggressive and females in heat are all best left at home.

If you do not intend to travel by car, your options will be limited. In many countries, trains and buses will not accept dogs as passengers or cargo, except those specially trained to assist people with a handicap. While most airlines do allow dogs to travel on board, they are usually required to travel in the baggage compartment if they are over 10 inches (25 cm) tall.

Consider your destination. Check that the campground or hotel you're going to allows dogs. Also, are you willing to involve your pet fully on your vacation? While dogs love to go camping, most don't enjoy being cooped up all day in a strange hotel room while their owners are out.

If you're traveling to another country, think long and hard before taking your dog, especially if it's only a brief trip. In many places a dog will be quarantined, sometimes for up to six months.

Traveling with your dog

If you feel your vacation would not be complete without your dog, by all means take him along, but make sure you prepare properly (see box right). To help prevent travel sickness,

HOME AWAY FROM HOME A special traveling case is ideal for carrying a small dog safely, whether you are making the journey by car, bus, train or airplane.

feed a light meal no later than six hours before the trip, and provide constant access to water. If this doesn't relieve

SAFETY RESTRAINT
This German Shepherd mix wears a harness that is tethered to an anchor point in the back of the car. Another way to stop a dog from leaping into the front seat and distracting the driver is to have a netting barrier fitted behind the front seat.

PREPARING FOR YOUR TRIP

- Have your dog checked by a vet before you go and ask about diseases you might encounter that your dog needs to be protected against.

Things to pack include:

- A first-aid kit.
- A current health certificate, proof of vaccination and medical history.
- Any medications your dog takes.
- Toys and a favorite bed or blanket.
- Your dog's leash and collar with an identification tag, and his license.
- A supply of your dog's regular food and treats to last the whole trip.
- Food and water bowls.
- Plenty of water.
- Grooming tools, including a flea comb and tweezers.
- Photos of your dog in case he is lost.
- Bags and scoops to clean up messes.

the nausea, ask your vet about medication for future trips.

Most dogs do not need tranquilizers when traveling. In fact, a tranquilized dog may have difficulty breathing when traveling in the baggage area of a plane. If you feel that your dog should be sedated, consult your vet. Always test tranquilizers at home before your trip.

Traveling by air Check with each airline because regulations and costs vary. Most airlines require health certificates signed by a vet within ten days of departure. The space allotted for animals is limited and reservations must be made well in advance. While some airlines may allow a small dog to travel in the cabin with you, larger dogs must travel in the baggage area. Either way, you must have a container approved by the airline.

To reduce the stress of flying try to book a non-stop flight and avoid traveling during peak travel times or extremes of weather.

Traveling by car Make sure that your dog is restrained. Dog seatbelts, crates and barriers prevent a dog from disturbing the driver and reduce the risk of injury from sudden stops or accidents. Try to follow your

DIETARY CHANGES

To avoid diarrhea and tummy upsets, take enough of the food your dog normally eats with you on your trip. If that is not possible, introduce his new food gradually by mixing increasing amounts with his usual food. This method also applies when you have to change his diet for other reasons.

CONVENIENCE Dry foods may be the easiest for traveling and many top brands are widely available. Ask your vet to advise you on the best choice for your dog.

pet's normal routine as closely as possible. Feed at his regular times, but feed less, as he will be less active while traveling. If carsickness is a problem, feed at the end of the day.

Never leave your dog inside a closed car on a warm day. The temperature inside a car can rise dangerously high within just a few minutes, and this often leads to heatstroke, which is potentially fatal (see p. 62). If you must leave your dog in the car, park in a shady area. Keep your dog restrained and open the windows and sun-roof as wide as you can.

BOARDING AND KENNELING

If you can't take your dog, you must decide where he will stay. If you can get someone to feed, walk and keep your dog company, he can stay right in his own home. Better still, try to get someone to live in your home while you're away. There are also reliable, insured pet-sitting services.

If this is not feasible, there are many reputable kennels that will take excellent care of your dog. To find a good one, get references from friends or your vet. Be sure

REGULAR PIT STOPS Pull over every few hours to allow your dog to relieve himself, stretch his legs, and drink some water.

to make a thorough tour of the facility, including the housing, feeding and exercise areas, before booking in. There should be someone on the premises at all times and a veterinarian should be available if needed. When you drop your dog at the kennel, leave a favorite bed or blanket and a couple of his toys. Having familiar things about will make the transition easier.

A HEALTHY DOG

Keeping your dog in good health means more than an annual checkup. Here's what to watch for.

Basic Care

YOUR DOG'S BASIC NEEDS ARE SIMPLE: love, food, exercise
and somewhere warm to sleep. She looks to you
to fill these needs in the same way that wild dogs look to
their pack leader to lead them wisely. The responsibilities
of pet ownership are great, but the love and friendship
you will receive in return are priceless. Just ask one of
the millions of happy dog owners who couldn't
imagine life without their canine friends.

FEEDING YOUR DOG

Like people, dogs require a varied diet, one that contains carbohydrates, protein, minerals, fat and vitamins. Your dog should also have fresh water at all times. This is necessary to maintain proper levels of body fluids, so that nutrients can be carried throughout the body and wastes can be eliminated.

VARYING NEEDS

A dog's nutritional requirements vary according to his age and level of activity. Working dogs have quite different requirements than more sedentary house pets.

GIVE-A-DOG-A-BONE Chewing bones can cause problems for your dog. Like this Boxer, she's probably better off with a Nylabone or a rawhide chew. Never allow dogs to eat chicken bones or cooked bones of any kind.

Likewise, pups or pregnant dogs have higher nutritional needs than older animals. Be sure to choose a dog food that is labeled "nutritionally complete and balanced" for your dog's lifestyle and stage of life. Most brands of dog food carry this information on the label. Don't overnourish your dog. Giving food that is meant for an active young dog to a seden-tary old one will not make him any healthier—just fatter.

TYPES OF DOG FOOD

Commercial dog foods come in three basic types: dry, semi-moist and canned. What you choose to feed your dog is up to you. All are nutritionally complete. The differ-

Daily Food Requirements

BODY WEIGHT	CALORIES/DAY	CANNED	SEMI-MOIST	DRY
5 lb (2.3 kg)	250	⅓–½ can	¾–1 cup	¼–¾ cup
10 lb (4.5 kg)	420	⅔–1 can	1½ cups	¾–1¼ cups
20 lb (9.1 kg)	700	1½–1¾ cans	2½ cups	1¼–2¼ cups
40 lb (18.2 kg)	1200	2–3 cans	4¼ cups	2½–3½ cups
80 lb (36.4 kg)	2000	3–5 cans	7½ cups	4–6 cups
100 lb (45.5 kg)	2400	4–6 cans	8–9 cups	5–8 cups

ence is in the ingredients, cost, palatability and convenience.

FOOD AND WATER BOWLS

Your dog will need her own bowls. If she has long, pendant ears, try to find the kind of bowl

TASTY SNACKS
Crunchy fresh fruit and vegetables will keep your dog's breath sweet and teeth clean.

designed for her breed, so she can eat and drink without dunking her ears. Flat-bottomed stainless-steel or ceramic bowls are more hygienic and less likely to slip or to spill than plastic bowls. Put the bowls either inside your dog's pen or close to her bed.

EXERCISING YOUR DOG

KEEPING BUSY A Kong toy stuffed with edible treats will keep this Staffordshire Bull Terrier entertained for hours.

The key to a happy, healthy dog is exercise. Dogs are naturally very active and playful. Their wild relatives spend much of the day hunting for food and defending their territory while the young learn the skills they need to develop by playing. Pet dogs, on the other hand, are given all the food they need (usually more), and are often confined to the house or yard for most of the day. As a result, they tend to get overweight, out of shape and lazy. Lack of exercise can also lead to boredom, which makes many dogs unhappy and destructive.

THE NEED FOR EXERCISE

All dogs enjoy play and exercise, but the actual amount and type varies according to their age, breed and state of health. Before buying a new dog, get to know the different breeds and the amount of exercise they need. Breeds such as the sporting, herding and working dogs need regular vigorous exercise. If you are too busy to take them for more than a short, daily walk, you would be better with a less active breed.

WHAT EXERCISE IS BEST

Walking is the best all-round form of exercise, providing muscle toning and cardiovascular conditioning. When walking a dog in public, always use a leash. An extendable leash will give your dog plenty of freedom to explore, but also gives you short-leash control when necessary.

In general, try to give your dog some type of exercise every day but always check with your vet first. He or she can check your dog for any health problems (such as heart and joint problems) that may be aggravated by exercise, and suggest a safe exercise regimen. Breeds that are prone to bloat should not be exercised immediately after meals.

If your dog is old, out of shape or has health problems, start with a 15-minute walk on a leash each day and gradually increase the duration. For young, healthy dogs, leash walks alone may not be enough. For these dogs, vigorous off-leash activities should be added. However, dogs should be allowed off the leash only if they obey commands and only in safe areas where regulations permit. If your dog likes to play with your friends' dogs, arrange to meet up.

Jogging or running is another way to exercise energetic, healthy dogs, but use common sense when taking a dog for a run. Never run with a dog under six months of age and avoid running on very hot days.

Playing games This is one of the best ways to both stimulate your dog's mind and provide vigorous

SOFT TOUCH Try to walk or run on soft surfaces to protect your dog's footpads.

exercise. Game playing also helps you to establish your leadership in an enjoyable way. Games of fetch with balls, frisbees or sticks are excellent ways to give your dog an effective workout without getting yourself too sweaty.

GROOMING YOUR DOG

Grooming sessions should always be enjoyable. Start with a gentle massage accompanied with praise. About once a month do your home health checks (see p. 52).

Start grooming from head to toe. Use a flea comb to check for fleas or ticks (see p. 54). Clean any discharge from your dog's eyes with a cotton ball moistened in lukewarm water. If your dog's ears are dirty or there is any sign of discharge, clean the ear flaps and ear openings with a cotton ball moistened with alcohol or mineral oil.

DIFFERENT TYPES OF COATS

Short smooth coats Using a bristle brush or a hound glove, first brush against the direction the hair lies. This will help remove any excess hair from underneath. Then, using the same tool, brush in the direction the coat lies to pick up loose hairs on the surface. A once-a-week brushing will keep shedding under control.

Short double coats Use a slicker brush or pin brush, and start by taking sections of your dog's coat and separating it with your hand so there is a parting where the skin is visible. Then use the brush to comb out the undercoat, brushing outward from the skin

Slicker brush

Hound glove

Wide-toothed comb

Soft bristle brush

BASIC EQUIPMENT To make grooming easier, buy the tools that are recommended for your dog's coat type.

as you do so. This is the best way to keep mats from forming in the thick undercoat. The undercoat is thickest at the neck and hind legs, and you can brush it straight out with your slicker in these areas.

Use the same brush to go over the top coat, brushing with the lie of the coat. Brush your dog twice a week, but more often during the shedding season. **Short wiry coats** The characteristic wiry coat requires a different type of handling from the

more traditional smooth and double coats. Use a slicker brush, medium-toothed metal comb and a stripping comb on this type of coat. Run the stripping comb lightly along the back of the dog,

DIFFICULT JOB A groomer tackles an Afghan's long straight coat by parting it in sections and brushing out from the skin with a pin brush.

thinning the overgrown wiry coat. Go easy at first—you can always remove more hair later, but you can't put it back. This thinning does not need to be done at every grooming session, only when the hairs on the very top of the coat (called the guard hairs) begin to protrude along the back.

After thinning out, brush your dog's wiry coat in layers, from the skin outward, with the slicker brush. Then comb in layers in the same way with a metal comb, to pick up any loose hairs.

Long double coats With a thick undercoat as its trademark, these are the coats that shed the most. Use a slicker brush or pin brush to brush the entire body first, taking sections of the hair and separating it with your hand. Brush outward from the skin to help remove the loose hairs in the thick undercoat. After this, take a wide-toothed comb and place it deep within the coat, parallel to the skin. Comb outward in this way to remove more loose undercoat. The undercoat is thickest on the back legs and also around the neck, so you may need to work through some mats here with a mat splitter.

Mat split

Long coarse coats The long, human-hairlike quality of this

CLEAN EYES Wipe the eyes from the outside toward the center with a damp cotton ball to remove muck and debris.

CLEAN EARS Use a damp cotton ball to wipe the ear canals clean, being careful not to pack any excess wax down further.

Pin brush

slicker brush, working in the direction the hair lies.

Curly coats These coats need regular brushing to keep the neat, curly look. To make the coat fluff up away from the body, brush it against the way it grows with a slicker brush.

coat means that it easily gets tangled and matted. Most pet owners have these coats clipped regularly to keep grooming to a minimum. Begin by removing any mats that you find, being careful not to break the hairs. If you sprinkle some cornstarch on the tangles, they will be easier to separate. With a pin brush, brush the entire coat out gently in the direction that it grows. Then go over it again with a soft bristle brush.

Long silky coats The biggest challenge here is dealing with the mats that form around the legs, ears, side of the face or anywhere else the hair is particularly long. To remove mats, use a mat splitter, then brush the entire coat with a

PAMPERING This Staffordshire Bull Terrier mix is having her sore feet treated to a soak in a dilute Betadine solution.

BATHING YOUR DOG

Unless they have rolled in something smelly, most dogs need a bath only once or twice a year. Brushing distributes the natural oils and cleans the coat much better than soap and water.

1. Try to give a bath on a warm day and start early. Thick coats, especially, take a long time to dry. First, brush the coat well to get rid of tangles—when a tangle gets wet it tightens up and is even harder to deal with.

2. If possible, use warm water and a shampoo made for dogs or babies. Keep suds and water away from your dog's eyes and ears. If possible, have someone to hold the dog still.

3. Rinse well—don't forget to rinse the feet well as soapy residues can make them itch. If possible, use a shower head on a flexible hose. Stand back when your dog shakes itself!

4. Use towels to dry the coat as much as possible. Let your dog run around to warm up. Brush its coat again to dry it quickly.

PENT-UP ENERGY When the bath is over your dog will rush about, shaking itself and trying to roll in the nearest bit of dirt.

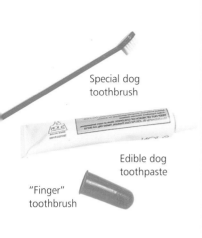

Special dog toothbrush

Edible dog toothpaste

"Finger" toothbrush

The best person to clip your dog's nails is your vet or a professional groomer. Dogs that walk on concrete regularly wear their nails down and so need less frequent trimming.

DENTAL CARE Ask your vet to clean your dog's teeth once a year. In between, rub them regularly with a "finger" toothbrush or a piece of soft towel over your finger. Use a dab of special dog toothpaste that is safe for your dog to swallow.

FOOTSORE To ease discomfort, spread the toes and trim the hair between them, following the line of each toe. Clean any dirt or discharge that has accumulated between the toes with a cotton ball moistened in warm water.

In Sickness
and in Health

USE REGULAR GROOMING SESSIONS to give your dog "home health examinations." Early detection of any physical health problems will help your veterinarian treat them more successfully. Start the examination by giving your dog a whole body massage. Begin with the head and neck area and gently progress down to the tail and feet. You will soon become familiar with what is "normal" for your dog and learn to pick up physical changes before they become problems.

A HEALTH CHECKLIST

Consult your vet if something in your home health examination doesn't seem right or if you notice any of the symptoms below.

WARNING SIGNS

- Loss of appetite for more than a day, trouble eating or mouth pain.
- Sudden loss or gain in weight, noticed by weighing or a rib check.
- Prolonged gradual weight loss.
- Pain and fever.
- Vomiting more than three times. Call vet at once if bloody or dark.
- Diarrhea for more than a day. Call vet immediately if bloody.
- Straining with bowel movements.
- Coughing or labored breathing.
- Sneezing for more than a day.
- Thirstiness for more than a day.
- Increased urination, sudden accidents in the house, difficult urination, straining, bloody urine or decreased urination.
- Excessive salivation.
- Sluggishness, unwillingness to exercise or behavior changes for more than a day.
- Excessive itching or scratching, ear rubbing or head shaking.
- Lameness for more than a day.
- Seizures or convulsions.
- Eye discharge, squinting or discomfort (a sign of pain).

Ears The ear canals should look clean, pink and free of discharge. Pain, swelling, unpleasant odor, tenderness or discharge means trouble.

Eyes The eyes should be bright and clear with no sign of discharge, redness, cloudiness or squinting (a sign of pain).

Teeth If the teeth are yellow or brown, they may need professional cleaning.

Mouth Carefully check inside your dog's mouth. The gums and tongue should be pink (some dogs have black pigment spots, which are normal). Paleness or change of color to red, blue or yellow is a sign of disease. Any lumps in the mouth are abnormal.

Pads and nails Look for cuts on your dog's pads or damage to the nails. Do the nails need trimming?

Breath If your dog has "doggy breath," there is probably some gum or dental disease. Kidney and digestive problems are also a possibility.

Breathing Notice your dog's breathing. It should be regular and comfortable. Dogs normally pant when they are hot, excited or stressed.

Skin Notice the skin under the fur. Normal skin is clean and has no flakes, scabs, odor or grease. Look for fleas, flea dirt (flea excrement and eggs, which look like coarse black pepper) or ticks.

Coat Run your hands through your dog's coat. Healthy fur is shiny and will not fall out excessively when you do this. Look for any bald spots.

Tail end Examine your dog's tail end. The anal area should be clean, dry and free of lumps. If the skin looks irritated, your dog may have diarrhea or the anal sacs may be blocked.

Legs and paws Check legs and paws. Feel for lumps or painful areas.

Fitness Feel for your dog's ribs and belly. If your dog is fit, you should be able to feel the ribs. Overweight dogs have an obvious fat layer. Underweight or ill dogs have very prominent ribs. A pot belly in an overweight animal may be normal, but not if the rest of its body is thin.

Stiffness Pick up the legs, one at a time, to make sure there is no pain or stiffness.

HOME CHECKUPS

Changes to the skin, probably the most common canine problems, are easy to see. They can be as mild as dryness or as serious as a severe infection. Signs of skin disease include hair loss, itchiness, dandruff, redness, odor, pimples, scabs and lumps. Severe itching leads to scratching, rubbing and licking, causing skin infections. If licking is confined to one area, a painful infection, called a "hot spot," can develop. If your dog is scratching and there are no signs of fleas, consult your vet.

Feet and nails Your dog's nails should just touch the ground, letting the toes stand together in a compact group. When they are too long, the nails cause the foot to spread out, making it difficult for the dog to walk comfortably or even normally. Long nails often get snagged on rugs, floor cracks, or clothing, and a torn nail can be nasty, bloody and painful. (See page 47, *Clipping nails*.)

While checking your dog's feet, look between the toes for hair mats, burrs, sores or ticks. And check the pads for any sign of cracking or cuts.

The mouth Many people assume that dogs have bad breath and dirty teeth. Nothing could be further from the truth. Your dog's teeth, all 42 of them, should be white and healthy. The

HOT SPOTS It's hard to see hot spots on dogs with dense, heavy coats, such as these Samoyeds, or other breeds with coats that are prone to matting.

gums should be a bright, bubble-gum pink, perhaps tinged with black, depending on the breed. Red gums and bad breath are early warnings of serious dental disease. Dogs should have their teeth cleaned every day, but once or twice a week is usually enough to prevent problems (see p. 47).

Dandruff This indicates dry skin. Add a little oil to your dog's food.

Obesity Dogs that put on too much weight soon start to feel uncomfortable. They also have a higher than average risk of developing diabetes and arthritis. Since dogs don't go from firm to fat overnight, it's important to check your dog's weight regularly to keep it from creeping up.

You don't have to weigh your dog to find out if she's getting too fat. You can do a quick check with your hands and eyes. Look at (and feel) her ribs. If you can't see or feel them, she's certainly overweight. Ribs that are too prominent, by contrast, could mean that your dog is under-weight. Your vet can help to correct either problem.

OPEN WIDE Prop your dog's mouth open with a tennis ball while you check teeth and gums or search for foreign objects.

HEAVY DUTY This English Setter's owner weighs himself with the dog and without to establish the dog's weight.

PARASITES

Some dogs scratch because they are allergic to things they have eaten, touched or inhaled, but parasites also cause many itches.

EXTERNAL PARASITES

Fleas These small, flat, hopping insects are by far the most common skin parasites that plague dogs. Their bites lead to itching, chewing and scratching, most notably on the back at the base of the tail. Many dogs are allergic to flea saliva and develop severe itching all over the body. Dogs may also acquire tapeworms from ingesting fleas.

To look for evidence of fleas, use either a fine-toothed flea comb or your fingers and search around for the insects under the fur in the rump area or between your dog's hind legs. Also look for coarse, black "flea dirt" (a combination of digested blood and flea feces) in the coat. Flea dirt will turn red if placed on a moistened tissue.

Because fleas live both on and off your dog at different stages of their life cycle, eradication can be difficult. For effective treatment you must eradicate fleas not only from your dog and other pets, but also from your house and yard. Start by bathing your pets (any dog shampoo will kill fleas). When dry, use a flea comb to pick up any stragglers. Launder your pets' bedding and thoroughly vacuum your house, discarding the bag afterward. Consult your vet for advice about products that are safe and effective against fleas.

NON-TOXIC Fine-toothed flea combs will pick up fleas in your dog's coat.

Lice These biting insects are visible as they crawl over your dog's skin. Their white eggs, called "nits," are also easy to see on your dog's hair. If your dog is scratching and you see either lice or eggs, ask your vet about a safe insecticidal shampoo. Dog lice are easy to get rid of and are not contagious to people.

Ticks Although a tick bite itself usually causes little or no skin irritation, the danger of ticks is in the diseases they carry, such as Lyme Disease and Tick Paralysis.

ONCE A MONTH

This chocolate Border Collie's fleas are being killed outright. Part your dog's hair and apply a product, such as Frontline or Advantage, to the skin at the back of his neck, the only place a dog can't reach to lick it off.

Ticks look like flat, brownish seeds, but can swell to the size of a small grape when engorged with blood. If you find any, remove them as soon as possible to reduce the chances of a disease being passed on.

First kill the tick by covering it with rubbing alcohol. Grasp the tick as close to the skin as

QUICK CHECKOUT If your dog has been romping through fields or woods, like this Beagle, check it all over carefully for ticks, especially on the head.

possible with tweezers then gently pull it out, making sure you remove the head. Try not to squeeze the tick when removing it. Many flea-killing products will also kill ticks, but there are also products specifically for tick prevention. For advice about what to use, consult your vet.

Mites These microscopic parasites live under the skin. Two of them, Demodex and Sarcoptes, cause mange. Demodex mites are found in the hair follicles of all dogs. At times, when a dog's immunity wanes, the mites multiply and cause hair loss. Most cases are resolved naturally, but some spread and develop into severe infections.

Unlike Demodex mites, Sarcoptes mites are highly contagious. They burrow under the skin, causing intense itching, crusting and hair loss, especially on the elbows and ears. People may also be bitten by these mites.

If your dog is suffering from hair loss or obvious skin irritation, your vet will be able to diagnose mites by examining a tiny scraping of your dog's skin under a microscope. Depending on the diagnosis, treatment may consist of baths or an oral or injectable parasiticide.

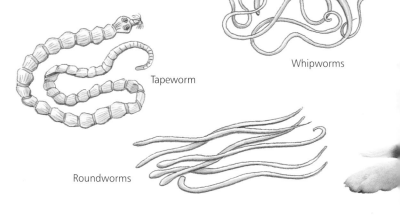

Whipworms

Tapeworm

Roundworms

GIVING A PILL

Take the pill between your thumb and finger and use your other fingers to push the lower jaw down. Put the pill near the back of your dog's tongue. Hold his mouth shut until he swallows. If he will not swallow, gently massage his throat.

INTERNAL PARASITES

Worms Intestinal worms and parasites are very common in dogs. Most cause few problems in their hosts, but are disconcerting for their host's owners. Sometimes you may see the adult worms in your dog's feces, but generally your vet will need to do a special microscopic examination of the feces to check if your dog has worms. Only then can the proper medication be prescribed to rid your dog of a specific type of worm. Fecal examinations should be a routine part of your dog's annual checkup.

ONLY NATURAL Unless their mother has been properly medicated, most puppies are born with worms or get them soon after through their mother's milk.

Visiting the Vet

Making sure that your dog lives a long and healthy life means providing not only a well-balanced diet and plenty of play and exercise, but also good preventive health care, starting in puppyhood. Ask your dog-owning friends to recommend a good vet or call your local humane society or veterinary association for a referral. At the first visit, your vet will give your puppy a thorough physical examination to make sure she is healthy, will set up a vaccination schedule for her and may check her feces for intestinal parasites.

Vaccination

Puppies are susceptible to several life-threatening, but easily prevented contagious diseases, such as distemper and parvovirus. Vaccines are given two or three times at three-to-four-week intervals until the puppy is 12 to 14 weeks old. The vaccines are given several times because most puppies carry temporary antibodies from their mothers that may interfere with their ability to develop their own protection. Most vaccines are boosted annually. Don't take your puppy to places where she will meet unvaccinated dogs until she has received all of her vaccines.

Depending on where you live and what your dog is likely to be exposed to, your vet may also recommend vaccines for the two strains of Leptospirosis (a disease transmitted by rats), rabies, viral hepatitis and Coronavirus, an

EYE CARE When there's debris in the eye, flush out the eye with saline solution. To spread eye ointment over the eyeball, massage the two eyelids together gently.

intestinal viral disease that can be serious for puppies. An intranasal form of a vaccine that prevents some types of kennel cough may be recommended for dogs that will be housed with other dogs (such as at dog shows or in boarding kennels).

SKIN PROBLEMS

Fortunately, the problem of hair-loss in dogs is usually treatable. It can be caused by parasites (mites), fungal infections, such as ringworm, or hormonal imbalance.

Redness, pimples and scabs, sometimes accompanied by bad odor and itching, may be signs of an allergy or a skin infection known as pyoderma. Your vet will probably prescribe antibiotics and special medicated baths.

A lump on or under your dog's skin could be a cyst, tumor or abscess. Cysts are usually painless and may be filled with fluid. Tumors vary in size and shape. Those with an unusual shape or color or that grow quickly may be cancerous. Abscesses (localized infections)

DROPS IN THE EARS

Holding the ear flap firmly to stop the dog shaking her head, squeeze the required number of drops into the ear. Maintaining your firm grip on the ear flap, massage the base of the ear gently to work the drops well into all the nooks and crannies.

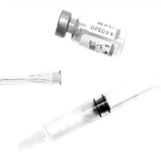

OTHER PREVENTIVE MEASURES Your vet may also suggest rabies shots, an oral heartworm preventive and protection from any problems that occur locally.

are painful and may burst of their own accord. It's best to have your vet check any lumps you find.

LICKING AND CHEWING

Licking is an effective way for your dog to remove dirt from her coat or soothe a scratch. But some dogs don't know when to quit. They lick and chew so often and for so long that they wear away the fur and damage the skin, causing sores and infections. Dogs often lick and chew their skin when they're feeling itchy— because of fleas, for example—or when they're in pain. They also lick when bored or stressed.

Start by treating for fleas (see p. 54). For dogs that are sensitive to fleas, even one or two bites can send them into a veritable licking and chewing frenzy. If the problem continues, distract your dog by giving her some attention. Then give her something else to chew, such as a rawhide or a chew toy. When dogs are licking themselves because of stress or boredom, this will help lift their spirits and keep their minds off their hides.

If your dog is licking at a sore or wound, she could interfere with the healing process and cause an infection. Wash small scrapes and scratches and treat them with an over-the-counter aluminum hydroxide preparation, such as those used for diaper rash or poison ivy. (Don't use products that contain zinc, which can be dangerous if your dog licks them off.) Also, apply an antibiotic ointment to prevent infection.

Allergies When pollen from garden or agricultural plants fills the air, your dog may go into frantic licking and chewing mode. The face, feet and backside are the areas itchy dogs usually chew at. Try keeping your dog indoors as much as possible on days when pollen counts are high, especially in the morning and evening. A cool bath gives instant, short-term relief from itching caused by allergies. A spritz of witch hazel spray is another instant soother.

Lick granulomas Dogs that focus all their licking energy on one spot of skin will sometimes develop serious, raised sores called lick granulomas. These usually appear on the lower legs between the elbow and the wrist and can be quite deep. They often

MAKING AN ELIZABETHAN COLLAR

1 In the center of a sheet of stiff plastic or cardboard, mark a circle with a circumference three inches larger than your dog's neck. Outside this circle, mark another with a diameter six inches larger than the first. Cut out the circles and remove a wedge.

2 Cut half-inch slashes around the inside circle and bend back the margin to form a rim. Punch lacing holes on each end of the collar.

3 Insert a lace into the holes and pull together—the circle will become a cone. Put the collar over your dog's head and tie the lace securely.

get infected, so you may need to bandage the area or fit your dog with an Elizabethan collar (see above). This will keep her from licking and give the sore a chance to heal. If the collar stops the licking but the sore hasn't healed in two weeks, see your vet. Better still, see your vet as soon as a problem starts to develop.

VITAL SIGNS

A dog's normal heart rate is between 80 and 140 beats per minute. The heartbeat can be felt by placing your hands around the chest just behind the elbow and gently pressing. To check for respiration, look for movement in the chest. If a dog is unconscious and appears lifeless, place a thread or hair in front of the nose to detect the slightest flow of air. The normal body temperature for a dog is between 100.5 and 102°F (38–39°C). To take your dog's temperature put a dab of lubricating jelly on the tip of a rectal or digital thermometer and carefully insert it about 1 inch (2.5 cm) into the rectum. Hold on to the thermometer firmly throughout and read it after two minutes.

Anything over 103°F (39.5°C) is a fever and deserves immediate veterinary attention.

The only sure way to tell if your dog has a fever is to take her temperature. Most feverish dogs have poor appetites, are inactive and have a "dull" look to their eyes. They tend to have warm, dry noses, but so do many healthy dogs, so your dog's nose is not a good indicator of a fever.

BASIC REQUIREMENT It's essential that your dog always has access to clean drinking water, but especially when she has a fever or diarrhea. Because this Boxer is in pain and reluctant to get up, his owner brings the water to him.

DEHYDRATION

If your dog has a fever, she won't feel hungry, but it's important that she drinks some water. If she does not, she can quickly become dehydrated, which is a serious problem. An easy way to check this is to take the skin on her back gently between your thumb and fingers and pull it out a little way. Do this a few times on a dog that isn't sick and you will see that the skin slips back into place quickly when you let go. When a dog is dehydrated, the skin slips back much more slowly. If your pet has diarrhea or is vomiting, she can become seriously dehydrated very quickly.

Heatstroke Never leave your dog in a car with all the windows wound up. The temperature inside a closed-up car can rise dramatically within just a few minutes, leaving your dog dehydrated and in a state of collapse. In this case, wrap her in wet towels, give her ice cubes to lick and take her straight to the vet.

SUNBURN PROTECTION

Collies, Shetland sheepdogs, and other dogs with little or no pigment in their noses are prone to a condition called, aptly, Collie Nose. Without pigment, the nose is very sensitive to sunlight, which can lead to painful burns. Some owners permanently tattoo these dogs' noses black, but this won't protect them from the sun. Wearing sunscreen and staying out of bright sun is the only way to keep their noses healthy.

LIMIT EXPOSURE Dogs with short white coats, such as this miniature Fox Terrier, should have sunscreen applied to the nose and belly to protect from sunburn.

Specialized
Care

- A First-aid Chart *66*
- Emergency Measures *68*
- The Older Dog *80*

AT SOME TIME OR OTHER, nearly every dog will get hurt, just because dogs are active, curious and never think about protecting themselves from injury. Usually, the injuries are relatively minor and you'll be able to cope with them at home. Other times, you will have to get your dog to a vet for expert advice and assistance, but you may need to give him first aid at home, before you put him in the car. The following solutions to common emergencies are easy to administer—even for the faint-hearted. This section also includes tips on making life easier for an older dog.

A FIRST-AID CHART

EMERGENCY	SYMPTOMS	TREATMENT
Unconscious dog	Dog is motionless but has pulse and heartbeat	• Clear airway and pull tongue forward (see p. 73) • Check for heartbeat or pulse • If you think that the dog may have any broken bones, handle it extremely carefully (see Suspected fractures)
Suspected fractures	Severe pain, dog not putting weight on leg	• Handle carefully to cause minimum disturbance • A small, calm dog can be lifted with both hands to support body. Keep back straight. If a limb is broken, let it dangle while supporting the body (see p. 68) • Place a larger dog on stretcher without twisting the dog's body (see p. 69) • Do not apply splint yourself
Shock	Dog is weak, cold to touch, has pale or grayish gums; breathing is rapid	• Let dog lie in comfortable position • Keep dog warm by loosely wrapping in a blanket or towel
Minor wound	Shallow breathing with only slight bleeding	• Snip away hair to expose the wound area • Clean with antiseptic • See your vet soon after to prevent infection
Deep wound	Gaping so underlying tissue or internal organs are visible; severe bleeding	• Control bleeding with pressure bandage made of gauze sponge or a piece of cloth (see p. 76) • If wound bleeds through wrap, add layers. If area can't be bandaged, apply direct pressure • DO NOT APPLY TOURNIQUET • Rush dog to vet, maintaining pressure on wound
Drowning	Dog is motionless in water	• Clean any discharge from the nose and mouth and pull tongue forward (see p. 73) • Hold dog by hind legs and gently swing to drain lungs of water (see p. 74) • If dog does not start breathing, start CPR (see p. 73)
Burns	Flame/hot oil or water comes into contact with fur or skin	• Cool burn area with cold water for 15 minutes while contacting the vet • Apply a cold compress

REMEMBER: *You are not an expert. Your goal should be to prevent further injury and to minimize pain and distress while seeking IMMEDIATE veterinary care.*

EMERGENCY	SYMPTOMS	TREATMENT
Electric shock	Collapse, loss of consciousness, inability to breathe, cardiac arrest, shock and burns to mouth	• Turn off appliance and disconnect cord before touching dog • Administer CPR if necessary (see p. 73)
Heatstroke	Heavy panting, red gums, weakness, collapse. Brain damage or death may follow if help is not sought	• Lower body temperature gradually with cool water to 103°F (39.5°C) • If ice packs are available, apply them to head and neck
Choking	Dog is in obvious discomfort, shaking head, salivating, gagging, putting paw to mouth. Gums may turn blue or pale gray and dog may collapse	• Look in dog's mouth. If you can see and grab object, remove it but be careful that the dog doesn't bite • With a small or medium-sized dog, hold it upside down and shake • If you can't dislodge the object, rush dog to your vet. If your dog has swallowed the object, X-rays and surgery may be required to remove it • Fish hooks can be removed from a dog's mouth or tongue by cutting off barbed tip with pliers. This may call for a tranquilizer and a vet's help
Poisoning	Twitching, excessive salivation, vomiting, nervousness, diarrhea, difficult breathing, change in pupil size	• Take dog to the vet immediately • If you know what the dog ate, take the container with you to show the vet
Seizure	Can be caused by brain tumor, brain injury, poisoning, epilepsy. Causes twitching, crying out, salivation, vomiting, emptying of bladder or bowel	• Don't put hands in or near dog's mouth —a convulsing dog has no control and may bite involuntarily. A dog won't swallow its tongue • It is best not to handle a dog during a seizure, but if you must move it, use a towel or blanket to protect your hands. Seizures usually end after a short while, but if they continue, take your dog to an animal hospital that can handle emergencies

REMEMBER: *You are not an expert. Your goal should be to prevent further injury and to minimize pain and distress while seeking IMMEDIATE veterinary care.*

EMERGENCY MEASURES

Knowing how to recognize and react to common emergencies may save your dog's life. But remember, it is vital that you seek immediate veterinary help.

Dogs are lively, curious and adventurous creatures and can quickly get themselves into all sorts of trouble. Unfortunately, it is common for dogs running free in urban areas to be hit by cars. This kind of traumatic injury can result in lacerations, fractures, shock, bleeding, spinal injuries, internal damage to the chest or abdomen and, sometimes, death.

While this situation is best prevented by keeping your dog leashed or confined to a fenced yard, sometimes a dog will escape and be hit despite your best efforts. If your dog is hit by a car, take him to a vet immediately. However, when you move him, make sure you do so carefully (see illustrations above right).

SUSPECTED FRACTURES

If you suspect a fracture, handle the dog so as to cause minimum disturbance. Remember that if

MOVING A SMALL DOG Using both hands to support the whole body, lift the dog carefully. Let the fractured limb dangle.

there has been a fracture of the spine, movement can lead to paralysis. Before transferring the dog, remove any mucus or foreign material from the mouth and pull the tongue forward to clear the airway. Do not attempt to splint a limb yourself as this may waste valuable time and cause the dog unnecessary stress. Get him to a vet immediately.

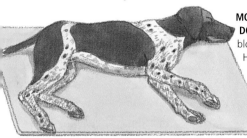

MOVING A LARGE UNCONSCIOUS DOG Check that the airway is not blocked before moving the dog. Handling him so as to cause minimum disturbance, carefully place him on a board or stretcher, without twisting the body. Get the dog to a vet immediately.

HOW TO MAKE A MUZZLE

When your dog is injured, or you are trying to help someone else's injured dog, the first thing you must do is muzzle him. If you don't have a shop-bought muzzle, fashion a makeshift version using your dog's leash, a pair of pantyhose, a necktie or a long strip of stretchable gauze. Even though it can be upsetting to see your dog trying to free himself, remember that the muzzle is there to help keep you both safe. Make sure your dog can breathe easily.

1 Tie a loose knot in the middle of the strip of material, leaving a large open loop.

2 Approach your dog quietly from behind and slip the loop over his snout. Pull the knot taut about halfway up his nose.

3 Bring the ends down and knot them under his chin. Carry the ends around his neck and tie again behind the ears.

BITES AND CUTS

Dog fights are a common cause of injury, particularly among male dogs. Bite wounds usually don't look bad and may not be bleeding at all, but looks can be deceptive. Bites often leave deep puncture wounds with narrow openings, which means that bacteria from saliva can be trapped inside. Such wounds can become infected very easily, and are best treated with oral or injected antibiotics prescribed by a veterinarian.

CUTS ON PAW PAD Bandage foot and wrist firmly, but not too tightly, leaving toes free so you can check for swelling.

While not emergencies, minor wounds should be cleaned carefully. Any wound to the eye or to any other sensitive part of your dog's body should receive immediate professional attention.

DEEP CUTS

Serious cuts—from glass or metal—don't happen often, but when they do you must act quickly. The first priority is to stem the flow of blood. Here's what you need to do:

Put it under pressure The best way to stop bleeding is to apply direct pressure to the wound. Use a clean handkerchief, towel or cloth, or even your hand. The bleeding should slow within a few minutes. If the towel is quickly saturated with blood, apply another one over the top, but don't remove the first one because you may break the blood clot that is forming over the wound. Keep pressing until the bleeding stops.

If the bleeding doesn't ease in a few minutes, apply pressure to one of your dog's pressure points—places where arteries are fairly near the surface of the skin (see p. 77). Pressing on a pressure point compresses the artery, inhibiting the blood flow to the wounded area. Serious bleeding is potentially life-threatening, so deal with it immediately and head straight for the veterinarian.

Clean it well Cuts on the paw pads less than about half an inch long can be treated at home. It's important to clean them well, preferably with a little antiseptic soap (such as a Betadine scrub).

Protect it Although wounds often heal faster when they're open to the air, a cut on a paw pad must be bandaged to stop it getting dirty and infected. Clean the paw, pat it dry gently, put a little antibiotic ointment on a gauze pad and place it over the wound.

If a small cut reopens when your dog walks around, wrap some gauze around the foot, continuing to bandage a little way up the leg. (Don't wrap the toes because you need to watch for swelling.) Pad the wound at least one-quarter to one-half inch thick with gauze. Wrap the gauze with first-aid tape, and change the bandage every 24 hours—sooner if it gets wet or starts to smell.

Cover the bandage To protect the bandage from dirt and moisture, put a plastic bag or sock on your dog's paw when he goes outside (remove it when he comes inside).

Wound inside the ear

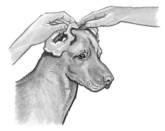

1 A wound inside a long floppy ear needs air to circulate around it, so fold the ears on top of your dog's head.

2 Secure the ears in place with a bandage wrapped under your dog's chin and tied on top of his head.

BURNS

Ever hopeful that you'll drop a morsel, dogs are often underfoot in the kitchen. While most stay out of trouble, some get a little too close to the action and suffer burns, especially from spattering grease or scalding water.

Heat burns Quickly putting ice on a burn or holding it under cold running water will help to ease the pain and stop further damage. The cold stops the heat of the burn from reaching the deeper tissues.

Cardiac massage

The easiest way may be the garden hose, provided you don't turn the faucet on full force. Help your dog to remain calm by talking to him continuously in a soft, soothing voice and by stroking him with one hand as you wet him down with the other.

With minor burns, the skin is red, tender to the touch and possibly swollen. Apply an antibiotic ointment twice daily, checking the skin carefully each time you reapply the ointment, to make sure the wound is not getting worse.

Deeper burns require immediate professional care. Place sterile gauze pads over the burned area, then apply an ice pack. If you don't have sterile gauze pads, use ice cubes in a

1 If the dog is unconscious and has no heartbeat, try cardiac massage. Place your hands on the chest behind the dog's elbow and press down gently but firmly (left). Repeat five or six times at one-second intervals.

2 Alternate massage with a breath (see mouth-to-nose resuscitation right). Try for at least 10 minutes.

plastic bag. At the same time, wrap your dog in a blanket to keep him warm and prevent shock. (A dog in shock has pale or grayish gums, rapid breathing and is weak and cold to the touch.)

Chemical burns Flood the area with water to dilute the substance and wash away any remaining chemical on the skin. Take your dog to the vet immediately.

APPLYING CPR

If your dog is unconscious, is not breathing and/or has no heartbeat, try cardiopulmonary resuscitation (CPR) and call your vet urgently. CPR calls for mouth-to-nose resuscitation (below) and cardiac massage (left). Remember the three rules, ABC: Airway (clear it); Breathing (establish airflow); and Circulation (cardiac massage).

MOUTH-TO-NOSE RESUSCITATION

1 After calling for veterinary help, remove any mucus or foreign material from the mouth. and pull the tongue forward to clear the airway.

2 If dog is unconscious, place your mouth over the nostrils and blow a steady stream of air for 2 to 3 seconds. If dog is small, place your mouth over the dog's mouth and nose.

3 Pause for 2 to 3 seconds to allow air to exit lungs. Continue until veterinary help arrives, or until normal breathing resumes, which may take as long as an hour. Check for a heartbeat and apply cardiac massage, if needed.

DROWNING

Follow the directions below to drain water from the lungs. If the dog does not start breathing, start CPR (see p. 73) and take your dog to the vet immediately.

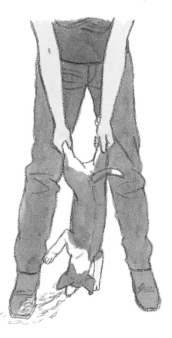

1 If dog is motionless, first clear any discharge from nose and mouth and pull tongue forward (see Step 1, p. 73).

2 To drain water from dog's lungs, hold the animal by its hind legs and gently swing it back and forth (above).

TEN SYMPTOMS TO WATCH FOR

There may come a time when your dog is seriously ill. Often, the warning signs will come on quickly. Other times, the problem will build up slowly over a few days. That's where knowing what's normal for your dog and what's not will pay dividends, alerting you to changes before they become an emergency. If your dog displays any of the following symptoms, seek immediate help from your vet.

Persistent or bloody vomiting or dry retching Dry retching can be a symptom of bloat, which occurs very quickly and is an extremely serious condition.

Sudden change of appetite or thirst could indicate a serious problem such as diabetes.

Rapid weight loss can be a sign of heart failure, diabetes, or liver or intestinal problems.

Any kind of bleeding, especially in urine or stools, may indicate a serious illness or trauma.

Significant change in urination habits could signal kidney failure, an infection, or poisoning.

Confusion, staggering, or collapse may indicate heart problems,

A BROKEN TAIL must be seen by a vet. If the break is not at the base of the tail, clean and dress the wound, then bandage a splint to the tail. Start at the tip and overlap layers closely to provide support, but not too tightly or you will cut off the blood supply.

brain problems, hormonal disorders, high blood pressure, or that a poisonous substance has been consumed.

Sudden persistent whining or crying indicates that your dog is in pain. Call your vet.

Difficult breathing may be caused by a foreign body obstructing the airways, or by heart and lung problems.

Weakness, lameness, lack of coordination could be a result of trauma, infection, or heart failure.

Persistent diarrhea could indicate a severe infection, poisoning, bowel injury, cancer, or an intestinal disease.

SCARY THINGS THAT AREN'T EMERGENCIES

Some things look worse than they are and can often be treated at home, or at least can wait if you can't see your vet right away.

A reverse sneeze sounds like a prolonged, repetitive snort. It's strange, but it's entirely normal.

Knee cap popped out of place occurs mainly in small and miniature dog breeds. It looks worse than it is. Call your vet, but it isn't an emergency.

Torn toenail Nails can get caught and torn on all manner of things. Torn nails bleed a lot, but are easy to treat at home or at the vet's.

Occasional vomiting It's not unusual for a dog to vomit occasionally because of stomach upsets, eating too quickly, or eating too much. However, if vomiting persists, see your vet.

Tapeworm segments around the anus These look like short grains of white rice and can be a little alarming the first time you see them, but they are easy to treat with medication that you can get from your vet.

BLEEDING

The sight of blood makes many people feel woozy, but when your dog is hurt and bleeding, you are his only lifeline. Take charge of the situation by talking to your dog in that soothing voice he knows and trusts—doing this will help you to stay calm as well.

Always act quickly if your dog is bleeding, but especially so if the blood is spurting from a cut. This generally indicates a cut artery, which bleeds more rapidly and causes heavier blood loss than a cut vein. Blood from a cut vein will ooze more slowly and evenly. To stop bleeding try these three methods in the following order: apply direct pressure to the wound, apply pressure on the pressure points and apply a tourniquet (only as a last resort).

Apply direct pressure Place a sterile gauze pad directly over the bleeding area and press down firmly. If you don't have sterile gauze, use a clean rag, cloth or your fingers until someone can get you bandages. If blood soaks through the dressing, don't remove it. Just add more layers to

Applying a tourniquet

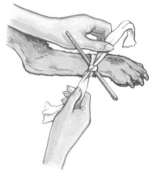

1 Apply a tourniquet only as a last resort. Wrap a strip of material twice around your dog's limb or tail, but don't knot it. Place a stick on top and tie it in place with the loose ends.

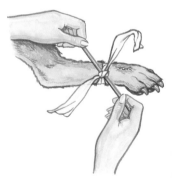

2 Turn the stick in one direction until the bandage is just tight enough to stop the bleeding. Loosen the tourniquet every five to ten minutes for a few seconds so that blood can circulate.

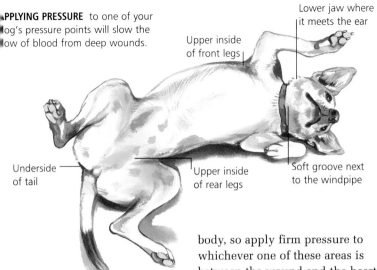

PPLYING PRESSURE to one of your
og's pressure points will slow the
low of blood from deep wounds.

Lower jaw where
it meets the ear

Upper inside
of front legs

Underside
of tail

Upper inside
of rear legs

Soft groove next
to the windpipe

he pile. This way, if clots have
started to form, you won't break
them apart. Once the bleeding has
stopped, remove the bandage and
pile of cloths, then use clean
material to bandage the wound. If
the bleeding hasn't stopped after
five minutes, bind the gauze pads
in place with tape so your hands
are free for the next strategy.

Apply pressure to pressure points
You may be able to reduce the
bleeding by clamping down on
the artery that supplies blood to
that area. There are five main
pressure points on your dog's
body, so apply firm pressure to
whichever one of these areas is
between the wound and the heart.
You should be able to feel a pulse
if you are over the right spot.
Always choose the point closest
to the wound. If bleeding
continues, let up on the pressure
slightly for a few seconds every
few minutes to allow some blood
flow to the surrounding area so
that healthy tissues aren't
damaged by being deprived of
their blood supply.

Apply a tourniquet If your dog is
still bleeding heavily after
pressure to his pressure points for
more than ten minutes, apply a
tourniquet as shown at far left.

POISONING

Serious poisoning is always an emergency and is scary. It happens quickly and by the time symptoms appear you may have only minutes to save your dog's life. Here's what to do:

- **Identify the poison** The more information you can give your vet, the faster he'll be able to start the appropriate treatment.

- **Smell your dog's breath** Petroleum products like gasoline and kerosene have a very strong and distinctive odor.

- **Check for bleeding** Dogs that are bleeding from mouth, nose, or anus may have eaten rat or mouse poison containing warfarin.

- **Look in the mouth** Check for acid burns or traces of the substance that has been eaten.

- **Search for the source** Quickly check house and yard for the remains of packages that may have held something poisonous. Check the bathroom and your purse for missing medications.

- **Check the ground for chemical spills** Dogs will often lap up hazardous substances such as antifreeze from puddles lying on the ground.

- **Check the pantry** Some human foods, especially chocolate, can poison dogs. Baking chocolate contains high levels of theobromine, a compound toxic to dogs. Just four ounces of baking chocolate can poison a 30-pound dog.

- **Take along the evidence** When you're pretty sure what your dog has swallowed, pack up what remains—or the package it came in—and take it with you to the vet. Product labels include vital information about ingredients and, in some cases, first-aid treatment. At the very least, if you give your vet this information, he will be ready when you arrive. Poisoning doesn't always cause vomiting, but when it does, be sure to scoop up a sample and put it in a plastic bag. Your vet may need to analyze it to figure out what, exactly, your dog has eaten.

- **Phone the poison experts** Keep the number of a 24-hour national animal poison center handy.

- **To induce vomiting** With a syringe, force a weak solution of hydrogen peroxide into your dog's mouth (about one tablespoon peroxide per 15 to 20 pounds of body weight), or use salty water.

When to Induce Vomiting

POISON	INDUCE VOMITING	POISON	INDUCE VOMITING
Antifreeze	Yes	Motor oil	No
Arsenic (ant, rat, mouse poison)	Yes	Nail polish	No
		Paint thinner	No
Aspirin	Yes	Paintbrush cleaner	No
Battery acid	No	Paste (glue)	No
Bleach	No	Pesticides (see arsenic, strychnine, warfarin)	
Carbolic acid (phenol)	No	Phenol (see carbolic acid)	No
Crayons	Yes		
Drain cleaner	No	Pine-oil cleaners	No
Fertilizer	No	Plaster	No
Furniture polish	No	Putty	No
Glue	No	Roach traps	Yes
Household cleaners	No	Shampoo	Yes
Insecticides (including flea and tick dips)	Yes	Shoe polish	Yes
		Sidewalk salt	No
Kerosene	No	Slug and snail bait	Yes (if bait has organo-phosphate carbamate, induce vomiting only if just eaten)
Kitchen matches	Yes		
Laundry detergent	No		
Lead (found in old linoleum, old paint, old plaster, old putty)	Only if eaten in last half hour	Strychnine (rat and mouse poisons)	Yes
		Toilet bowl cleaners	No
Medications (heart pills, vitamins tranquilizers, antihistamines, amphetamines, barbiturates)	Yes	Turpentine	No
		Warfarin (in rat poisons and medications)	Yes, but only if just eaten
		Weed killers	Yes

THE OLDER DOG

It can sometimes be hard to tell whether changes you notice in your pet are due to a medical problem, a behavioral problem or a combination of the two. While you can't turn back the clock, there is a lot you can do to help your dog enjoy her senior years.

Anticipate some changes. It's not unusual for older dogs to become less responsive or to forget their training. So don't assume your dog is deliberately ignoring you when she doesn't respond to your call or she just stands there when you tell her "Sit." Those surprise puddles in the house could be because she's lost muscle tone or has an infection or other medical problem. Or maybe she just forgot she had to go outside. Extra toilet training isn't going to help here.

AGING SENSES

Your dog's eyesight may fade, she may not hear as well as she once did, and even her sense of smell may be somewhat impaired. Your dog will accommodate and adjust to this gradual process, so much

CATARACTS are a common problem, particularly in older dogs. They make the center of the eyes look opaque or white. Severe cases may benefit from surgery.

so that you may not even notice at first. But be considerate of your older pet and her set routines. Any sudden changes could be stressful or confusing. If you have to move the furniture or do a major remodeling and your dog's eyesight isn't what it used to be, take her on a tour of the new layout rather than have her bump into things.

Keep her walking Your dog will benefit from regular exercise and njoy it as much as she always as, although the pace will probably be slower. While she might be old in years, you want to keep her feeling young in spirit and exercise is a great way to keep her alert and interested in what's going on around her.

Feed her right A good, balanced diet will work wonders for your older dog, but there's no need to switch her to a special diet unless your vet specifically says to do so.

Be careful not to overfeed her. It's important that she doesn't become obese, as this can lead to a number of health problems. **Ask your vet** about supplements rich in antioxidants, such as vitamin C and vitamin E, which help combat some of the deterioration that aging can bring. An older dog may also need more B vitamins to help the kidneys work more efficiently. Your vet will give your dog a complete physical examination and run tests to check for any disorders common in elderly dogs.

Your dog will have her own health needs. Pay close attention to her and how she's getting along. Plan her meals and activities with this in mind, and she will enjoy a happy and healthy retirement.

CHECK HER BREATHING This mixed breed cattledog sits quietly while her owner listens to her chest.

Breeding

IF YOU ARE GOING TO BRING NEW DOGS into the world, aim to improve the standard of the breed. Every dog that is bred should represent an improvement, in some way, over its parents. In general, it is best to avoid breeding mixed-breed dogs. The overpopulation of dogs is a huge problem and shelters are already full of unwanted mixed breeds, not to mention purebred dogs. Unless you can guarantee a good home for each and every puppy you breed, you will only be contributing to the problem.

CHOOSING A MATE

To ensure that the pups you breed will be of the best quality, choose your bitch's mate with great care. Don't pick a neighborhood dog that will perform for free! Read up on canine reproduction, pregnancy, birth and postnatal care. Although dogs were once bred for specific tasks, most are now kept as companions. Never breed with a dog that is aggressive, or overly timid. Choose a mate with the qualities of a good companion.

Choose a mate carefully Select a good representative of your breed from a reputable and responsible breeder. Make sure he is healthy and doesn't have any hereditary diseases. Make sure that both dogs are registered with a national kennel club, but remember that registration alone does not vouch for the quality of a dog. Have both dogs examined by a vet, including blood tests, X-rays and eye exams by a specialist and a check for parasites. In particular, ask your vet to check for hereditary disorders that are common in your breed. If brucellosis (a sexually transmitted disease causing sterility) is a problem in your area, have the dogs checked specifically for this.

CASE FOR NEUTERING

As adorable as puppies are, there are far too many of them. Each year, thousands of dogs are put to sleep in animal shelters because no one wants them. Many of these dogs are the result of accidental breeding. The only way to halt this tragedy is to stop allowing our pets to breed, and the safest and most effective way to achieve this is to neuter. By not adding to the population of dogs, the chance that homeless pets will find homes is increased.

With current veterinary methods, neutering of both sexes is relatively safe and painless. Furthermore, the potential health benefits are significant. Discuss this with your vet.

WHELPING

Most bitches do not need help to give birth. Interfere only in an emergency. Too much interference may cause your dog to become nervous and prevent her from properly caring for her newborns.

During delivery, your bitch may either stand or lie down. When the first puppy arrives, generally head first, it will be wrapped in placental membranes. The mother usually tears these off and eats them. At this point the pup will take its first breath. The mother then bites off the umbilical cord and eats the placenta, or afterbirth, which normally follows a few minutes later. Make sure that the bitch has expelled an afterbirth for each puppy. If she retains any, she may develop an infection.

Soon after birth, the pup will find its own way to the mother's nipple. If it doesn't, gently point the puppy in the right direction. The colostrum (or first milk) contains antibodies that protect newborns from disease.

PUPPY DEVELOPMENT In the first few weeks of life, puppies change from tiny, helpless creatures with closed eyes to fat, squirmy little bundles already showing individual personalities. At one week old (left), the eyes are still closed and the puppy sleeps a lot. At three weeks old (below), it can focus its eyes and move around. At six weeks, most are ready to leave their mothers. At four months old (right), it is full of fun and eager to explore its world.

SOCIALIZATION OF PUPPIES

Socializing your puppy means getting him used to people, other dogs, places and things. Between 3 and 10 weeks of age is a critical time in a dog's life. Your puppy needs to be exposed to the world outside so he can learn how to live happily with all that goes on around him. He needs your steady guidance.

OUT AND ABOUT

Taking your puppy with you when you visit a friend socializes him. So does meeting strangers while out for a walk, playing with another puppy, or examining a soccer ball. Your puppy needs to meet dogs of all sizes, and all types of people: senior citizens, toddlers, bearded men, women in sun hats, teenagers on skateboards and people pushing strollers. He needs to walk on carpet, grass, pavement and linoleum. He also needs to learn to climb steps (start by placing him on the third or fourth step and letting him walk down) and to ride in the car.

Two cardinal rules Never pet your puppy when he's afraid and always praise him for being brave. When your puppy seems fearful, do not reassure him with petting and soothing words because he will interpret your actions as praise. He will repeat what he is praised for over and over, so a

LEARNING BY PLAY
Your dog learns the important skills involved in relating to people and other animals during sessions of play, especially with other dogs. A big expanse of dirty water just adds to the fun of a game of chase for these three Salukis.

hesitant stance could become his learned reaction to anything new. On the other hand, never jerk him toward an object he fears. Such treatment could turn a little trepidation into total terror.

Link noise with niceness If loud noises make your puppy nervous, make a clatter mixing his meal in a metal pan with a metal spoon. Don't make a racket; keep the volume realistic. He'll soon learn that noise isn't necessarily scary.

Set an example If your puppy is afraid to go near something, leave him where he is and go yourself. Handle the object as if it were a winning lottery ticket and invite your puppy to join you. Sitting down beside the feared object works well. Your puppy will probably start creeping over, but hold your praise until he at least touches the thing with his nose. If the object isn't breakable or too large, roll it away from, never toward, your puppy. This might entice him to chase the object.

Ask a friend to help If your puppy is afraid of people, have a friend toss a dog treat his way.

A FRIENDLY WORLD If your puppy has good experiences as he begins to learn about the world, he will grow up confident and outgoing.

She should then ignore him and chat with you. When your pup approaches, your friend should kneel down. When your puppy comes in for an exploratory sniff, your friend should hold her hand low, reach under the puppy's chin and tickle him on the chest. Reaching over his head could make him back up in fright. If he doesn't approach, don't force him; give him a lot more socialization.

OBEDIENCE

Well-behaved dogs are welcome anywhere. Whether or not they do tricks, dogs with good manners always get the love they deserve.

Behavior

IF YOUR DOG HAS A TENDENCY toward bad behavior,
don't despair. With a bit of firm and consistent training you
can correct her naughty habits. Better yet, you can curb
unwanted behaviors before they become established habits
by starting to train your dog as soon as you bring her home.
Knowing the motivation for bad behavior is the key to
changing it. If your dog doesn't have enough things to
keep her busy, then she'll find her own entertainment,
however unappealing an activity it may seem to you.

Common Problems

The key to changing unwanted behavior is to recognize what is motivating and maintaining the behavior. What follows are some common problems and ways to combat them.

Jumping up Many pet owners complain about their dog jumping up on them or visitors. But owners often inadvertently reinforce this behavior. If your dog is allowed to jump up in certain situations and not in others, it's very difficult for him to understand when jumping is acceptable and when it is not. Furthermore, jumping up usually gets attention—even if that attention is just pushing the dog away—and this may be enough to maintain the behavior.

For young animals, pushing may be interpreted as a signal for play. Crouching down to greet your pup is a good way to start training him not to jump. If you want your dog to jump up on you for petting, teach him to do this on command, so the behavior is under your control. To eliminate unwanted jumping behavior

successfully, you need to identify any and all reinforcement for the behavior. If the jumping up occurs when you come home, pay him no attention until he sits calmly.

Keep your dog on a leash when greeting people, or practice "sit" and "stay" in the doorway of your home. Get people he knows to approach him with a toy kept handy for the purpose—he gets the toy only if he does not jump up. What is important is patience and practice, including greeting less familiar people. In order for your dog to learn, he should always sit to be greeted, even by members of the family.

Barking Dogs bark for many reasons—to communicate, to indicate excitement and to alert people to intruders. It is vital to correctly identify the motivation of a dog that barks excessively.

Some dogs are left alone all day and their barking drives the neighbors crazy. This is very difficult to stop and you should look at why the dog must be left alone. It may be possible to find him a suitable backyard buddy. If your dog is barking while you are home, and you are not able to make him stop, teach him a "quiet" command. Yelling doesn't help—he'll just think you're barking back in reply. You must establish a clear association between your command and the desired response (see box below).

As a last resort, bark collars that use a noise deterrent or those that use a citronella spray may be effective, but shock collars are not recommended.

Teaching "Quiet"

To train a dog to stop barking, you must first get it to start. So, use something that will reliably get the dog to bark, such as the doorbell.

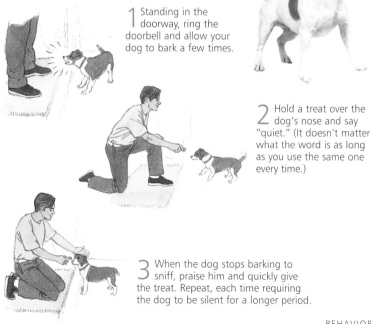

1 Standing in the doorway, ring the doorbell and allow your dog to bark a few times.

2 Hold a treat over the dog's nose and say "quiet." (It doesn't matter what the word is as long as you use the same one every time.)

3 When the dog stops barking to sniff, praise him and quickly give the treat. Repeat, each time requiring the dog to be silent for a longer period.

Aggression In dogs, aggression includes growling, barking, snarling, lunging, snapping and biting. Sometimes a dog will indicate its aggressive intentions by staring and standing tall with its ears and hair erect. Fear and nervousness are also likely to make a dog behave in an aggressive manner.

The best way to deal with aggressive behavior is to prevent it in the first place. If you get a new puppy, establish yourself as his leader from the word go. Do this by setting rules that are humanely but consistently enforced. Get your new pet used to you handling his food, his toys and his body. Do this when he is calm rather than when he is excited by exercise or play.

Reward good behavior with treats and praise. If you need to take something from your puppy, do so in a firm but gentle manner and offer him something else in its place. If you yell and reach quickly for your pet, you may scare him and prompt aggression in return. Remember, harsh punishment can cause aggression based on either fear or pain.

If aggressive behavior occurs a number of times, you may need to seek help from a qualified behavior therapist. Do not assume that your pet will grow out of the behavior. Aggression is serious and potentially dangerous.

Who's the boss? Most dogs intrude on people's space because they have learned that they're rewarded—they are petted and reassured. Some do it for another reason: to put you off-balance. Dogs use physical contact not only to express affection but also to establish pecking order.

A dog that shoves, hip slams, or leans against other dogs—or

YOUR SPACE OR MINE? Dogs that want to take over the couch aren't just trying to get comfortable. They may be making a bid for "top dog" status in the house.

people—is establishing a position of authority. A dog that shoves past your legs when you open the door or tries to take up more space on the couch by leaning against you is essentially trying to establish dominance.

Digging Dogs dig for many reasons. Some, such as terriers, were bred to dig out small animals. Try setting aside an acceptable digging spot in your yard. This can be of a different

PEOPLE FIRST Being first in line for dinner is a sign of status among dogs. This terrier mix doesn't like waiting her turn, but she's learning that people have higher status than she does. Don't give food for free. A subtle way to teach dogs to be less aggressive about food is to remind them that you control it. Do this by taking their food away sometimes and then giving it back.

material, such as sand, or can be surrounded with wood. Then bury things there that your dog would like to dig up.

BODY LANGUAGE

ON GUARD DUTY This Border Collie's full attention is on something out of the ordinary. It's her job to alert her owner, so her stance is confident, her eyes focused. She'll continue to bark until her owner assures her that everything is now okay.

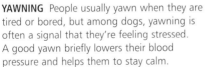

YAWNING People usually yawn when they are tired or bored, but among dogs, yawning is often a signal that they're feeling stressed. A good yawn briefly lowers their blood pressure and helps them to stay calm.

THE PLAY-BOW This is the way your dog invites either you or another dog to join in a game. When a dog wants to play, it will lower the front half of its body to the ground. The rear end will be left pointing in the air in what looks like a bow, and the tail will be waving madly in anticipation. The head may be lowered, with the mouth and lips relaxed, and the dog may pant. Sometimes it will give a high-pitched bark and prick its ears up alertly. The ears may point forward or, if they are pendant ears, be held as high and as far forward as possible. When the play invitation is answered, the dog will bounce up and down and may bark in excitement. Once play is under way, the exuberant body language expresses happiness.

SIDEWAYS LOOK A stare isn't always a sign of aggression. Dogs look out of the corners of their eyes, as this German Shepherd mix is doing, when they're being coy or asking to play. It's a polite way of expressing interest without being pushy. On the other hand, if they're watching the cat, for example, but want the cat to think they're asleep, they may stare with their eyes almost closed.

FEAR OF THUNDERSTORMS
Dogs' senses are much sharper than ours. They hear, smell and sense things with a clarity that we can hardly imagine. Because they hear higher and lower frequencies than we do, the sound of thunder is more intense and scary. Then there are the changes in atmospheric pressure that accompany storms, and the gusting winds that bring sudden changes in airborne scents. When thunderstorms are raging, this Australian Shepherd follows his natural instinct and looks for shelter in an enclosed place, such as under the bed, where he will feel safer.

TUCKED TAIL Submissive, anxious, or frightened dogs, like this Chihuahua, invariably tuck their tails between their legs. The farther the tail is tucked, the stronger the feelings. A very frightened dog will tuck his tail right under his stomach. But even when the tail is tucked, the tip will wag a bit, which displays his stress. In puppies, a tucked tail shows respectful submission when greeting adult dogs. Once the adult accepts a young dog's greeting, the tail will uncoil and start moving more naturally again.

TAIL WAGGING Although a wagging tail, like this Labrador's, usually indicates a friendly dog, that's not always the case. Dogs also wag their tails when they are scared, agitated or unsure. A frightened dog may wag her tail low and between her legs as she decides whether to fight, flee or go belly up. An aggressive, angry dog may wag her tail high while she chases or even attacks. Look at what's going on— is the dog's best buddy just getting off the school bus, or is another dog eating out of her dish? Also check how the dog has distributed her weight—an aggressive dog's body will be tense and the weight will be mainly on her front legs.

Training

For dogs that love food, a great way to teach
new tasks is to use food as the reinforcer, coupled with
praise. Other dogs may respond better to a toy, playtime
or praise alone. It is very important that food rewards
are used randomly once the behavior is learned, although
they should not be eliminated altogether. The goal is to
make these food rewards unpredictable. On the other hand,
give verbal praise with or without a food reward
every time your pet performs correctly.

TEACHING GOOD BEHAVIOR

Teach Your Dog "Sit"

1 Find a reward for your dog, such as a small treat. After getting his attention and showing him the reward in your hand, move your hand up and over his head.

2 As he follows your hand with his eyes, his rear will naturally drift toward the ground and he will automatically sit. Say "sit" as he completes the sit, praise him lavishly and give him the reward.

Teach Your Dog "Stay"

1 With your dog sitting or lying down, show her the flat of your palm, with your fingertips pointed up. Say "stay" and smile as you move back one step. Return immediately, praise your dog, and give her a reward.

2 Repeat, but this time move two steps back. Slowly increase your distance from your dog, and the length of time she must stay. You can also put her leash on and give a very gentle tug while telling her to "stay." She will soon understand exactly what you want her to do. Slowly increase the distractions by introducing background noise and having people moving around near her.

Teach Your Dog "Lie Down"

Your dog doesn't need to be fluent in sign language to learn how to respond to common hand signals. Most dogs can learn basic signals in a matter of minutes.

1 Put your dog in a sitting position. Hold a treat in front of his face. Move your hand down to the ground and back toward you a few inches. The path your hand follows should trace an L.

2 As your dog follows your hand with his eyes, his head will be lowered and he will lie down. When he does, reward him with the treat and lots of praise.

TOP TIPS FOR TRAINERS

- Choose a reward that really motivates the dog. (Use rewards that he regards as special: premium food items and toys reserved for play as part of training.)
- Don't expect the dog to guess what you want him to do. Take small steps that allow the dog to build the behavior you want.
- Reward the dog for even very small improvements. Once he is responding reliably, withhold the reward until you see another small improvement.
- Watch the dog when you reward him: if he wags his tail, that's good; if he does not wag his tail, you need to make the exercise more fun.
- Never punish a dog that is trying to get a reward; withhold the reward until you see a response you like.
- As an individual trainer or a family of trainers, be consistent in your use of verbal commands, and in delivery of rewards for improvement.

Teach Your Dog "Come"

1 Start by facing your dog, who should be a few feet away. Have your hands at your sides and a treat in your hand. Say your dog's name and the word "come." As you say "come," sweep your arms up and out to the side.

2 Then sweep your arm or arms forward and into your chest. If your dog doesn't respond to the hand signal and verbal command, use the treat or run back a few steps to lure her to you.

Teach Your Dog "Heel"

"Heel" means "stay by my side when we go walking." Some dogs are natural heelers, while others require a lot of training. To teach your dog how to go out for a stroll with you without taking you for a mad dash, use his training collar and a loosely held six- or eight-foot leash. Be prepared to spend a lot of time outdoors because this exercise can't be practiced inside.

1 Have your dog on a loose leash on your left side. Hook your right thumb into the loop of the leash and hold it with your right hand so that it crosses your body. Keep your right hand at your waist.

2 As you start walking with your dog, say his name and the word "Heel." If he doesn't pay attention and follow you right away, use your left hand to give the leash a gentle tug backwards.

3 If he starts to pull or lag, touch the leash gently with your left hand and turn in the opposite direction. If you bump into him, don't apologize. It's his job to stay out of your way.

4 He'll soon learn to keep a watchful eye on you. When your dog is walking nicely by your side, look at him and praise him verbally. You can also reach down and give him a pat.

Teach Your Dog "Roll Over""

Watching a dog roll over on command looks like magic but it's actually one of the easiest tricks to teach your dog. All dogs can do it, but the smaller in size they are, the easier it is for them to roll. Very large dogs, such as Irish Wolfhounds and Great Danes, may take more time to train. When your dog can do this really well, you can use hand signals to indicate which side you want her to roll to.

1 Give your dog the "Down" command. Kneel beside her and place one of your hands on her outer thigh and the other on her inner shoulder.

2 As you gently roll her away from you, say "Over," in a confident tone of voice.

3 When she completes the turn and jumps to her feet, make a big fuss over her. Repeat this exercise a few times a day until she can roll over without your help.

Teach Your Dog "Fetch"

Fetch is a fun game for both you and your puppy, and will provide your pet with much of the exercise he requires. Some dogs will fetch more eagerly than others as certain breeds, such as retrievers, naturally pick things up and carry them around. The hard part is getting them to give them back.

1 Toss a toy or ball a short distance. When the puppy looks to the toy, say "fetch."

2 As the puppy picks it up, say "good dog" and "come."

TOILET TRAINING

Your puppy is most likely to eliminate immediately after waking or playing, or within 10 to 20 minutes after eating. Take him outside at these times and last thing at night to the place that will be his permanent toilet area. Don't take the dog inside until he has finished (take an umbrella, if necessary). When he "performs" for you, praise him. The focus of house-training should be teaching your puppy where to "go." Eventually, he should learn that this means outside. Don't be surprised if he has an occasional lapse. Toilet training takes time and patience, so don't give up.

3 To get your puppy to drop the toy on command, hold up another toy and say "drop it."

4 When your puppy drops the toy, praise him and quickly throw the new toy. His main reward in this game is that the game continues.

Teach Your Dog "Drop It"

When your dog starts chewing on your credit card or a project you've left on the desk you don't want to start a game of chase to get the item back. Even if you manage to catch up with your dog, you'll be hard pressed to rescue your possession by prying her mouth open. Once she lowers her head and decides to clamp her jaws down, you're in for a battle. Instead, teach her to "Release" or "Drop it." This command is also useful for when your dog gets hold of dangerous objects or spoiled food.

1 Start with your dog on the leash. Command her to sit in front of you and give her something she can hold in her mouth. It should be large enough for you to be able to grasp part of it while she has it in her mouth.

2 While your dog is holding the object in her mouth, say "Hold" and praise her for a few brief moments.

3 Hold the leash two feet from her collar and jerk it downward, telling her either to "Release" or "Drop it." At the same time, use your other hand to grasp the object firmly, but don't pull it out of her mouth. Offering a food treat at this point is the easiest way to get her to release her grasp. Then guide the object gently out of her mouth.

4 Praise her lavishly when she releases it. It may take a few tries before she follows this command easily. Keep repeating the exercise until your dog drops the object quickly, then test her with other objects. Be sure to praise her so she knows she's done well.

SHOWING

Dog shows are either restricted to one breed of dog (known as specialty shows) or are all-breed shows. At either type of show, judges first examine and evaluate each dog for overall structure, fitness, coat color and quality and temperament. They then evaluate each dog's gait, or movement, by watching it move around the ring.

In most countries, the breeds are divided into classes, generally based on age, for the initial round of competition. The winners of each class then compete against each other as well as with dogs that are already champions. The judge then picks the "best of breed." If the competition is an all-breed show, the best of breed winners then compete against all others in their group (for example, sporting or herding dogs). Finally, the "best in show" is chosen from the winners of each group.

Most dogs at shows compete for points that will eventually qualify them as champions (designated by the letters Ch. in front of the dog's name). The number of points a dog can win at a show varies from one to five depending on a variety of factors, including the number of dogs at the show and the dog's breed and sex. For a dog to qualify as a champion it must win 15 points under at least three different judges, including at least two scores of three points or more (known as "majors").

CONFORMATION SHOWS

Conformation simply means conforming to a breed standard (a description of the perfect example of a given breed). Purebred dogs

SHOW CLIP This Lowchen has been given a "lion clip," most often seen on Poodles, to show off its best features.

re judged on how closely they measure up to their breed standard. Conformation shows are restricted to unneutered, purebred dogs. Some people choose to handle their dogs themselves at the shows, while others prefer to hire professional handlers.

OTHER COMPETITIONS

If formal dog shows sound a little out of your league (or your dog's), there are other types of events where both neutered animals and mixed breeds are eligible. These include obedience trials, tracking tests, hunting trials, herding trials and agility competitions.

Obedience trials test the ability of both dog and handler to perform a specific set of exercises. Tracking tests require a dog to follow a trail by scent. Hunting trials test a dog's hunting ability in the field, while herding trials require a dog to control livestock in a variety of difficult situations. In agility competitions, dogs and handlers negotiate an obstacle course consisting of tunnels, inclines, seesaws and hurdles,

at high speeds. Whatever your interests, a dog show can bring out the best in your dog.

"STACKING" means placing a dog in the correct pose to show off its best features. This Alaskan Malamute is being correctly stacked, with its head to the owner's right, back straight and head and tail up.

BREEDS

The classification of dogs into groups varies from country to country. This guide to breeds uses the United States system.

Toy Dogs

MINIATURE DOGS WERE DEVELOPED by ancient
Chinese emperors as palace companions and lapdogs,
and they have remained popular with royalty through
the ages. These days they are popular pets, particularly
in cities, where their size, gentle temperament and
relatively low need for exercise make them
very suited to apartment living.

Chihuahua

Size: male 6–9 in (15–23 cm)
female 6–8 in (15–20 cm)

Weight: male 2–6 lb (1–3 kg)
female 2–6 lb (1–3 kg)

■ ABOUT THIS BREED
Little is known about the
Chihuahua (pronounced chu-wah-
wah) before its discovery about
100 years ago in Mexico, although
the breed is believed to date back
at least to the ninth century.
There are two distinct coat types:
smooth and short, or long. The
dogs are otherwise identical
and can occur in the same litter
(but in Britain, the two are
considered separate and never
interbred). Every coat color and
color combination occurs.

■ TEMPERAMENT
Intensely loyal, the Chihuahua
becomes very attached to its
owner, even to the point of being
quite possessive. When strangers
are present, it follows its owner's
every move, keeping as close as
possible. It learns quickly and
responds well to training.

Gold and white female
Shorthaired Chihuahua

Red and white
female Longhaired
Chihuahua

◼ GROOMING

The smooth, shorthaired coat should be gently brushed occasionally or simply wiped over with a damp cloth. The long coat should be brushed daily with a soft bristle brush. Bathe both types about once a month, taking care not to get water in the ears. Check the ears regularly and keep the nails trimmed.

◼ EXERCISE AND FEEDING

Although it is tempting to carry these dainty creatures about, they will keep fitter if taken for walks.

The tiny Chihuahua is the smallest breed of dog in the world.

It is safer to use a body harness than a collar. Feed small amounts twice a day, and avoid meat-only diets, despite the dog's demands.

SNAPSHOT

PERSONALITY **Affectionate, playful, alert, but may snap when afraid**
GROOMING **Regular brushing**
EXERCISE **Regular, gentle**
ENVIRONMENT **Ideal for apartment living, not suited to live outdoors**
BE AWARE **Reasonably healthy, but suffers from genetic eye problems, collapsing trachea, dislocating kneecaps and heart disease**

Pekingese

Size: male 7–10 in (18–25 cm)
female 7–10 in (18–25 cm)

Weight: male 7–11 lb (3–5 kg)
female 8–13 lb (4–6 kg)

■ ABOUT THIS BREED
Venerated since ancient times by the Chinese, the tiny Pekingese is, perhaps, the ultimate lapdog. These fabled dogs once led a pampered life in the Imperial Court of Peking, where the smallest specimens were often carried around in the capacious sleeves of royalty.

This is one of the few breeds in which the female is heavier than the male. The extravagant, long, straight, flowing coat has profuse feathering and comes in all colors, except albino and liver. The face is flat with a dark, wrinkled muzzle and drooping, heart-shaped ears. These tiny, bow-legged dogs have a characteristic rolling gait.

■ TEMPERAMENT
Although small, Pekingese are excellent watchdogs. They are loyal, alert, courageous and good tempered, and will adapt well to the family routine.

■ GROOMING
Daily combing and brushing of the very long, double coat is essential. Take extra care around the hindquarters, which can easily become soiled and matted. Females shed the undercoat when in season. Dry shampoo regularly.

Silver-gray brindle
male Pekingese

PERSONALITY **Devoted, determined**
GROOMING **Special care is needed**
EXERCISE **Regular, gentle**
ENVIRONMENT **Ideal for apartment living, not suited to live outdoors**
BE AWARE **Subject to breathing problems, like other short-nosed breeds. The large, prominent eyes are very sensitive, and prone to corneal ulcers and injury**

Clean the face and eyes daily—the eyes are vulnerable to injury and to corneal ulcers. Check the hairy feet for burrs and objects that may become stuck there.

■ EXERCISE AND FEEDING

Pekingese are disinclined to take walks and, although they don't need much exercise, they will stay in better health if given regular sessions of play activity. There are no special feeding requirements, but Pekingese will quickly become obese if overfed.

The Pekingese may have breathing problems that require surgery to correct. They also often encounter difficulty when giving birth and should be under the care of a veterinarian at this time.

Papillon

Size: male 8–11 in (20–28 cm)
female 8–11 in (20–28 cm)

Weight: male 3½–10 lb (1–5 kg)
female 3½–10 lb (1–5 kg)

■ ABOUT THIS BREED

The origin of the Papillon (French for "butterfly" and pronounced pah-pee-yon) is uncertain, but by the sixteenth century it had become a breed cherished among the European nobility. Because of the long, plumed tail, which is carried curled over the back, the Papillon was once called a Squirrel Spaniel. Its long, lustrous coat is white with patches of any color, except liver. The "butterfly" ears are heavily fringed and there is a well-defined white noseband.

■ TEMPERAMENT

Intelligent and adaptable, these animated little dogs have perky, friendly natures, but tend to be quite possessive of their owners. As watchdogs, their usefulness is limited by their tiny size, but they will alert you to unusual noises or to the arrival of strangers.

■ GROOMING

Daily combing and brushing of the long, silky, single coat is important and fairly straightforward. These dogs are usually clean and odorless. Bathe or dry shampoo when necessary. Keep the nails clipped and have the teeth cleaned regularly because they tend to accumulate tartar.

Red, sable and white male Papillon

These two charming Papillons steal hearts with their amusing antics and love to be the center of attention.

■ EXERCISE AND FEEDING

These playful little dogs love to go for a run but won't fret too much if confined to the house for days at a time. Like any dog, they benefit from a regular exercise regimen. Note that they are small enough to wriggle through fences that might appear to be secure. No special feeding requirements.

Pomeranian

Size: male 7–9 in (18–23 cm)
female 7–9 in (18–23 cm)

Weight: male 3–5 lb (1.5–2 kg)
female 4–6 lb (2–3 kg)

■ ABOUT THIS BREED

The Pomeranian resembles the much larger sled-pulling Spitz-type dogs from which it is descended. It was deliberately bred down in size during the nineteenth century, when toys and miniatures were very popular.

This little dog looks like a walking powderpuff of black, gray, blue, orange, cream, shaded sable or particolored hair. Its small, cheeky, fox-like face peers out from an outsize ruff. The spectacular tail is carried curled over the back.

■ TEMPERAMENT

Easy to train, the happy little Pomeranian makes a good watchdog, despite its tiny size. It will alert you to anything unusual by setting up a commotion of barking. Although excitable, it is obedient and easily calmed.

■ GROOMING

Frequent brushing of the very long, double coat is desirable. If you work from the head, parting the coat and brushing it forward, it will fall neatly back in place so, although time-consuming, the task is relatively easy. The cottony undercoat is shed once or twice a year. Dry shampoo when needed.

PERSONALITY Lively, loyal, friendly
GROOMING Frequent brushing
EXERCISE Regular, gentle
ENVIRONMENT Ideal for apartment living, best kept indoors
BE AWARE Subject to eye problems and susceptible to dislocated knees. Some animals lose their teeth as they get older. Barking can become a problem

Orange and sable male Pomeranian

The lively Pomeranian loves to play.

Clean the eyes and ears daily and take the dog for regular dental checkups to avoid loss of teeth.

■ EXERCISE AND FEEDING
There is no need to make special provision for exercise if there is a small area for the dog to play in. Otherwise, a session of play in the park from time to time will suffice. No special feeding requirements for this breed.

Yorkshire Terrier

Size: male 7–9 in (18–23 cm)
      female 7–9 in (18–23 cm)

Weight: male 4–7 lb (2–3 kg)
         female 3–7 lb (1.5–3 kg)

■ ABOUT THIS BREED

Developed only about a century ago to catch rats, the popular Yorkshire Terrier is a mysterious blend of various terriers: English, Scottish and Maltese. The Yorkies we see today are much smaller than their forebears.

The ultra-long, fine, silky coat parts along the spine and falls straight down on either side, although many owners opt for a natural shaggy look. The coat is steel-blue on the body and tail, and tan elsewhere. Puppies are usually black and tan. The tail is usually docked to half its length.

■ TEMPERAMENT

Alert, indomitable and spirited, the Yorkshire Terrier is also admired for its loyalty. Despite its diminutive size, it makes an excellent watchdog, defending its territory in no uncertain manner.

■ GROOMING

For show purposes, there are many tricks to caring for the Yorkshire Terrier's long, single coat, and strict guidelines must be adhered to. Even for the ordinary pet owner, grooming represents quite a commitment in time and effort. Daily combing and brushing and regular

hampooing are necessary to keep
he lustrous hair in top condition.
 is also important to keep the hair
ut of the dog's eyes. Alternatively,
onsider having your Yorkie
lipped. The teeth should be
caled regularly by a veterinarian.

EXERCISE AND FEEDING
.lthough it doesn't need a lot of
xercise, this lively little warrior
vill benefit from regular opportu-
ities to run and play. No special
eeding requirements, but restrict
he amount of meat in the diet.

ark steel-blue male
orkshire Terrier

If the dog is not for showing, many
owners opt for a natural shaggy look,
as seen in this young Yorkshire Terrier.

SNAPSHOT

PERSONALITY **Alert, brave, feisty**
GROOMING **Daily, extensive**
EXERCISE **Regular, gentle**
ENVIRONMENT **Ideal for apartment living, best kept indoors**
BE AWARE **Subject to eye problems, including cataracts, progressive retinal atrophy and dry eye, as well as deterioration and dislocation of hip and knee joints**

Japanese Chin

Size: male 7–11 in (18–28 cm)
female 7–11 in (18–28 cm)

Weight: male up to 9 lb (4 kg)
female up to 9 lb (4 kg)

■ ABOUT THIS BREED

These gorgeous little dogs have been known in Western countries for only about 150 years. However, they were the pampered pooches of wealthy Japanese, including royalty, for many centuries, having been introduced to Japan from China in ancient times. They are probably distantly related to the Pekingese.

The Japanese Chin looks like a tiny toy. The profuse, straight, longhaired coat comes in white with markings either of black or shades of red. The gait is graceful with the dainty feet lifted high off the ground.

■ TEMPERAMENT

The engaging little Chin is a lively, happy, sweet-tempered animal, the perfect size for small living spaces. With its gentle ways and charming manners, it is perhaps

The typical sweet-faced little Japanese Chin has a well-rounded skull.

Black and white male Japanese Chin

est suited to homes in which there are no small children. Because of its size and gentle nature it is of very little use as a watchdog.

GROOMING

Although the coat looks as though it might be difficult, a few minutes each day will keep it looking beautiful. Comb out tangles and brush lightly, lifting the hair

lightly to leave it standing out a little. A professional dog groomer can show you how to do this correctly. Brush a dry shampoo through the coat occasionally and bathe only when necessary. Clean the eyes every day and check the ears regularly for any signs of infection. Matted hair must be clipped off the feet.

■ EXERCISE AND FEEDING

While they don't require a great deal of exercise, Chins love a daily walk and an opportunity to play in the open. There are no special feeding requirements, but they prefer to "graze" on small meals and tidbits. Don't let them overeat and become obese.

Maltese

Size: male 8–10 in (20–25 cm)
female 8–10 in (20–25 cm)

Weight: male 6–10 lb (3–5 kg)
female 6–10 lb (3–5 kg)

■ ABOUT THIS BREED
Celebrated since Roman times and perhaps even earlier, the gentle Maltese is featured in many famous paintings. It was specially favored by women through the ages. With its compact little body, short legs and silky, dazzlingly white coat, this dog is sure to be the center of attention. The oval eyes are large and dark, with black rims. The profuse single coat falls long and straight, parting along the spine and eventually reaching the ground, concealing the legs and feet completely. It is always white, sometimes with lemon or beige markings. The tail arches gracefully over the back.

■ TEMPERAMENT
Intelligent and easy to train, the Maltese enjoys being groomed, petted and fondled. Lively and alert, it will let you know by barking if strangers are about.

■ GROOMING
Daily combing and brushing of the long coat is important, but be gentle as the coat is very soft. Apply sunblock along the hair parting to prevent sunburn. Clear the beard after meals to prevent staining. Clean the eyes daily for the same reason (a smear of

PERSONALITY **Even-tempered, affectionate, playful**
GROOMING **Regular, extensive. Be gentle with the soft coat**
EXERCISE **Regular, gentle**
ENVIRONMENT **Ideal for apartment living, not suited to live outdoors**
BE AWARE **Generally long-lived, hardy and healthy, but subject to genetic eye diseases**

Two Maltese siblings play in a snug basket.

White male Maltese

petroleum jelly on the tear channels will reduce yellowing). Bathe or dry shampoo regularly, making sure the animal is thoroughly dry and warm after a bath. Clean the ears regularly and ask a professional groomer to pull out hairs growing inside the ear canal. The hair on the top of the head is often tied up in a topknot to stop it from irritating the eyes.

■ EXERCISE AND FEEDING

Maltese enjoy a regular walk or session of frolicking in the park and they remain playful well into old age. There are no special feeding requirements for these dogs, but avoid overfeeding.

Shih Tzu

Size: male up to 11 in (28 cm)
female up to 11 in (28 cm)

Weight: male 10–18 lb (5–8 kg)
female 10–18 lb (5–8 kg)

■ ABOUT THIS BREED

These entertaining little dogs love company and like nothing better than to sit on your lap and be groomed. A number of striking similarities suggest that the Shih Tzu (pronounced shidzoo) is descended from Tibet's Lhasa Apso (see p. 290), possibly as a result of being crossed with the Pekingese after it was introduced into China. The Shih Tzu is also known as the Chinese Lion Dog or the Chrysanthemum Dog.

This is a proud-looking little dog with a long body and short legs. The thick, long, luxuriant coat can be any color, but a white blaze on the forehead and a white tip on the tail are very desirable.

■ TEMPERAMENT

Endowed with loads of character, the gentle, loyal Shih Tzu makes friends easily and responds well to training. As you would expect with a dog this size, they make only an adequate watchdog.

■ GROOMING

Daily combing and brushing of the long, soft, double coat with a steel comb and a bristle brush is essential, with extra care during molting. The long hair on the top

of the head is usually tied in a topknot to keep it out of the dog's eyes. Dry shampoo as necessary and bathe once a month. Check the ears regularly for infection and remove food scraps from the beard after meals. Clip out any matting on the feet.

■ EXERCISE AND FEEDING
These are naturally active little dogs but, if allowed, like to lounge about in their own particular spot. They should be encouraged to get out and about and will keep fitter with a daily

Like other floppy-eared breeds, the Shih Tzu is prone to ear infections, because air circulation is reduced by the abundance of hair around the ears.

Gold and white male Shih Tzu

walk. There are no special feeding requirements, but don't overfeed or they will quickly become fat.

SNAPSHOT

PERSONALITY Friendly, playful, loyal, independent
GROOMING Extensive
EXERCISE Regular, gentle
ENVIRONMENT Ideal for apartment living, not suited to live outdoors
BE AWARE Eyes are prone to injury and can get dry from exposure, causing them to ulcerate. Also subject to inherited kidney problems

Toy Poodle

Size: male up to 11 in (28 cm)
female up to 11 in (28 cm)

Weight: male 6–9 lb (3–4 kg)
female 6–9 lb (3–4 kg)

■ ABOUT THIS BREED

The Toy Poodle is the smallest of the Poodles (see p. 298), dogs originally used in Germany and France as retrievers of waterfowl. Later, the Toy was favored by circus performers for its comic appearance and because it was easy to train. It is the perfect pet for an older or less active person with time to pamper it.

This active little dog has a dense, woolly coat of springy curls. The hair keeps growing and is not shed and, for this reason, the Toy Poodle is often found very suitable as a pet for people with allergies. The coat comes in solid red, white, cream, brown, apricot, black, silver and blue.

■ TEMPERAMENT

Sensitive and remarkably intelligent, the Toy Poodle is highly responsive and very easy to train. It makes a very good watchdog for its size.

■ GROOMING

Poodles must be bathed regularly and clipped every six to eight weeks. Clean and check the ears frequently for wax or infection and have a professional groomer pull out hairs growing inside the ear canal. The traditional clips

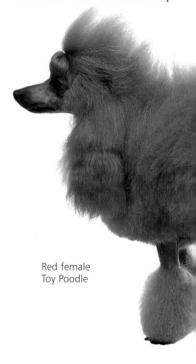

Red female
Toy Poodle

PERSONALITY Very intelligent,
loyal, lively
GROOMING Comb and brush daily
EXERCISE Regular, gentle
ENVIRONMENT Ideal for apartment
living, not suited to live outdoors
BE AWARE Subject to dislocated
knees, epilepsy, diabetes and
genetic eye diseases, such
as progressive retinal
atrophy and cataracts

When buying a Toy Poodle puppy, check older relatives for any genetic disorders.

were developed to lighten the weight of the coat for swimming and protect the joints and major organs from cold, but many pet owners opt for a plain lamb clip, the same length all over. The teeth need regular scaling by a vet.

■ EXERCISE AND FEEDING
Toy Poodles are not demanding as far as exercise goes, but they love to go for a walk, and will keep fitter if given regular opportunities to run free and play. There are no special feeding requirements.

Pug

Size: male 12–14 in (30–36 cm)
female 10–12 in (25–30 cm)

Weight: male 13–20 lb (6–9 kg)
female 13–18 lb (6–8 kg)

■ ABOUT THIS BREED

Not at all pugnacious, this lovable
softie is good with children.
Pugs love company, but they will
sulk if left out of family activities.
Although dogs very similar to
Pugs appear on ancient Chinese
porcelain and paintings, the
origin of the breed is shrouded in
mystery. They seem to have been
house dogs or pets rather than
dogs bred for any particular task.

While not exactly handsome,
the Pug, nevertheless, has a
certain appeal. It has a square,
thickset, stocky body with a sleek,
soft coat that comes in fawn,
apricot, silver and black, all with
black muzzle and velvety ears.
The moles on the cheeks are
regarded as beauty spots. The tail
lies in a tight curl, or even, in the
best specimens, a double curl on
the back. The jaunty, rolling gait
is quite distinctive.

TEMPERAMENT

Intelligent, easily trained, and with a big bark for its size, the Pug makes a good watchdog. It is playful, loyal and affectionate and makes a captivating companion that will shadow your every move or curl up on your lap.

Fawn male Pug

■ GROOMING

Brush and comb the smooth, short coat with a firm bristle brush, and shampoo only when necessary. Clean the creases on the face regularly. The Pug's prominent eyes are prone to injury and other problems associated with poorly fitted eyelids.

■ EXERCISE AND FEEDING

Strong dogs with short straight legs, Pugs enjoy energetic games and will keep in better health if given regular exercise. (The short muzzle contributes to chronic sinus and breathing problems.) Don't overfeed, as Pugs will overeat, quickly become obese and live much shorter lives.

Chinese Crested Dog

Size: male 9–13 in (23–33 cm)
female 9–13 in (23–33 cm)

Weight: male up to 12 lb (5 kg)
female up to 12 lb (5 kg)

■ ABOUT THIS BREED
If you like the unusual, this may be the pet for you. It is not known how or where the Chinese Crested Dog originated, but it seems to have existed in ancient China. The breed has many similarities to the Mexican Hairless.

There are two distinct varieties of this unusual dog: one is hairless, except for its head, feet and tail, and called, not surprisingly, the Hairless; the other, the Powderpuff, has a coat of long, soft hair. Both come in numerous colors, either solid or mixed, or all-over spotted. Strangely, the two types often occur in the same litter.

■ TEMPERAMENT
Chinese Crested Dogs tend to become very attached to their owner and have difficulty adjusting to a new one. They crave constant companionship. Being small and shy, they do not make very good watchdogs.

■ GROOMING
Daily combing and brushing of the long, fine, double coat of the Powderpuff is important, with

White female
Hairless Chinese
Crested Dog

PERSONALITY Lively, devoted

GROOMING Powderpuff needs daily brushing

EXERCISE Regular, gentle

ENVIRONMENT Ideal for apartment living; not suited to live outdoors or in a cold climate

BE AWARE The skin may be allergic to contact with wool and must be protected from sunburn

White male Powderpuff Chinese Crested Dog

extra care required when the dog is molting. The woolly undercoat becomes matted if neglected. Bathe the Hairless frequently and massage a little oil or cream into the skin to keep it supple. Also protect the skin from sunburn.

■ EXERCISE AND FEEDING

Although these dogs enjoy a brisk walk, they will be just as happy with regular sessions of play. There are no special feeding requirements, but do not overfeed them, as they will quickly become obese if given the chance.

Cavalier King Charles Spaniel

Size: male 12–13 in (30–33 cm)
female 12–13 in (30–33 cm)

Weight: male 10–18 lb (5–8 kg)
female 10–18 lb (5–8 kg)

■ ABOUT THIS BREED
A fearless, lively little dog with a cheerful disposition, the Cavalier King Charles Spaniel is friendly and sociable with both people and other dogs, and is far more hardy than the average toy breed. Developed from a cross between a King Charles and a Cocker Spaniel (see p. 174), the Cavalier differs greatly from its forebears. Its breeders were trying to reproduce a toy dog similar to those seen in portraits from the time of England's Charles II—he was said to dote on these animals.

Compact and handsome, the Cavalier is slightly larger than the King Charles and has a longer muzzle, but comes in the same colors: solid reds, chestnut and white, black and tan, and tricolored black, tan and white. The coat is long and silky and free of curls, although it can be wavy. The ears are long, silky and well feathered.

■ TEMPERAMENT
The Cavalier is easily trained, clean and sensible, and makes a delightfully playful and diverting companion. It will let you know if strangers are about.

Chestnut and white male Cavalier King Charles Spaniel

■ GROOMING

The smooth, longhaired coat is easy to groom. Comb or brush with a firm bristle brush, and bathe or dry shampoo as necessary. Always make sure the dog is thoroughly dry and warm after a bath. Check the eyes and long, well-feathered ears carefully for any signs of infection. Trim the hair between the paw pads.

Teach Cavalier King Charles Spaniel puppies from the time they are very young not to nip and bite during play.

SNAPSHOT

PERSONALITY **Lively, friendly, playful, charming**
GROOMING **Regular brushing**
EXERCISE **Regular, gentle**
ENVIRONMENT **Ideal for apartment living, not suited to live outdoors**
BE AWARE **Heart disease is very common; also subject to hereditary eye diseases and dislocating kneecaps. The ears are prone to infection**

■ EXERCISE AND FEEDING

Whatever exercise you can provide will be just fine with this adaptable dog, although it does enjoy a good romp in the park. No special feeding requirements.

Italian Greyhound

Size: male 12–15 in (30–38 cm)
female 12–15 in (30–38 cm)

Weight: male 6–10 lb (3–5 kg)
female 6–10 lb (3–5 kg)

■ ABOUT THIS BREED

The graceful Italian Greyhound has been known since ancient Egyptian times. Whatever its original purpose, perhaps to flush birds, chase small game or kill rats, it has been bred for the past few centuries purely as a pet. It is usually classified as a toy breed.

Lithe and streamlined, these dogs are capable of short bursts of speed. The glossy, satiny coat comes in various shades of fawn, cream, white, red, blue, black and fawn, and white can be splashed with any of these colors.

■ TEMPERAMENT

As it tends to be timid and must be handled very gently, this is a good pet for a quiet household where there are no lively children. In stressful situations it needs constant reassurance by stroking. Not a good watchdog.

■ GROOMING

This dog is one of the very easiest to groom. All that is needed to keep the fine, silky coat gleaming is a rubdown with a piece of rough toweling or chamois. If absolutely necessary, the animal

Fawn male
Italian
Greyhound

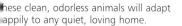

hese clean, odorless animals will adapt
appily to any quiet, loving home.

can be bathed, but make sure it is
thoroughly dry and warm after. Do
not expose to extremes of weather.

■ EXERCISE AND FEEDING
These active little dogs love to
run free and play as well as have
regular walks. There are no
special feeding requirements.

Terriers

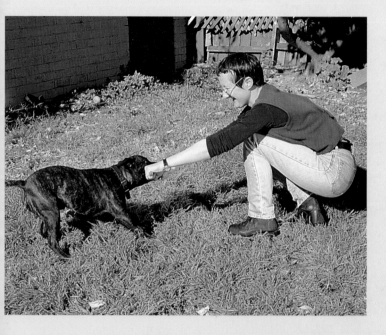

ALL TERRIERS HAVE MUCH in common. They were developed
mainly in the British Isles over the past few centuries,
although records exist of small hunting dogs from earlier
times. They are generally small, short-legged dogs, bred to
hunt small game, often by digging it out of burrows. They
are brave and determined, with powerful jaws to hold prey.
Long-legged terriers, such as the Airedale, were bred to hunt
larger game. Much of their aggression has been bred out, but
terriers remain playful, exuberant and incorrigible diggers.

Cairn Terrier

Size: male 10–13 in (25–33 cm)
female 9–12 in (23–30 cm)

Weight: male 14–18 lb (6–8 kg)
female 13–17 lb (6–8 kg)

■ ABOUT THIS BREED

The vivacious little Cairn Terrier will delight you with its antics and steal your heart with its courage and fun-loving ways. It makes an ideal pet, adaptable, friendly and alert. One of the oldest of the terriers, it has passed on attributes to many varieties through cross-breeding in the Scottish Highlands, where it originated. There it hunted among the cairns that dot the landscape.

This compact little animal has a hard, shaggy, weather-resistant outer coat that comes in cream, wheaten, red, sandy, gray, brindle, black, solid white or black and tan, with ears and mask often darker. The thick undercoat is soft and furry.

■ TEMPERAMENT

A strong, companionable and fearless dog, the Cairn Terrier is always ready to play or be petted. Energetic and always on watch, it will alert you to the presence of strangers by its growling and on-guard stance. Cairn Terriers are intelligent and easily trained.

■ GROOMING

That shaggy "natural" look actually takes quite a bit of maintenance and a neglected coat

Red wheaten
female Cairn
Terrier

oon becomes a sorry, matted ness. Brush several times a week, eing gentle with the soft ndercoat. Once a month, bathe he dog and brush the coat while t dries. Trim around the eyes and ars with blunt-nosed scissors and lip the nails regularly.

EXERCISE AND FEEDING
This dog will get enough exercise unning around a small garden, ut if you live in an apartment, it vill need a daily walk or a romp n the park. There are no special eeding requirements.

Light brindle female Cairn Terrier

SNAPSHOT
PERSONALITY **Alert, frisky, friendly**
GROOMING **Regular brushing**
EXERCISE **Regular, moderate**
ENVIRONMENT **Ideal for apartment living, but loves regular outings**
BE AWARE **Generally a healthy breed, but prone to allergy problems of the skin and subject to dislocating kneecaps and hereditary eye diseases**

Jack Russell Terrier

Size: male 10–15 in (25–38 cm)
female 9–14 in (23–36 cm)

Weight: male 15–18 lb (7–8 kg)
female 14–17 lb (6–8 kg)

■ ABOUT THIS BREED

Admired for its courage and
tenacity, the Jack Russell Terrier
will take on all challengers.
Although still not universally
recognized as an official breed,
the Jack Russell Terrier has been
around for about 100 years. It
takes its name from the English
"hunting parson" who developed
the dog. It was specially bred to
have the speed, stamina and
agility to hunt foxes.

This tough little dog is clean
and a convenient size for a house
companion. The coat may be
either smooth and short, or rough
and a little longer, and comes in
white, or white with black, tan or
lemon markings.

■ TEMPERAMENT

Jack Russell Terriers are happy,
excitable dogs that love to hunt.
In fact, they'll chase just about
anything that moves. They make
vigilant watchdogs, but can be
scrappy with other dogs. Smart
and quick witted, they must be
firmly trained from an early age.
They settle well into family life
and make devoted pets.

■ GROOMING

Both smooth and rough coats are
easy to groom. Comb and brush

Tan and white
female rough coat
Jack Russell Terrier

■ EXERCISE AND FEEDING

The Jack Russell Terrier is very adaptable and will exercise itself in a small garden, but it is in its element with space to run, hunt and play. Young dogs should be allowed to play with other dogs as much as possible in order to become well socialized. No special feeding requirements.

egularly with a firm bristle
rush, and bathe only when
eally necessary.

Tan and white female smooth coat Jack Russell Terrier. These brave little dogs will keep your property free of small interlopers, such as snakes.

West Highland White Terrier

Size: male 10–12 in (25–30 cm)
female 9–11 in (23–28 cm)

Weight: male 15–18 lb (7–8 kg)
female 13–16 lb (6–7 kg)

■ ABOUT THIS BREED

With similar ancestry to the other Highland working terriers, especially the Cairn Terrier, the "Westie" was selectively bred for its pale coat so as to be highly visible in the field. It was formerly known as both the Poltalloch and Roseneath Terrier.

This is a sturdy little terrier with an all-white coat and bright, dark eyes. The ears are small, pointed and erect, giving the animal an alert, ready-for-anything look. The tail is often carried at a jaunty angle and should not be docked.

■ TEMPERAMENT

Friendly, playful, alert and self-confident, this dog just loves companionship. It is bold, strong and brave, and makes a very good watchdog, despite its size.

■ GROOMING

The harsh, straight, shorthaired double coat is fairly easy to groom and sheds very little. Simply brush regularly with a stiff bristle brush. Brushing distributes the natural oils and should keep the coat clean, so bathe only when necessary. Trim around the eyes and ears with blunt-nosed scissors. The whole coat should be trimmed about every four months and stripped twice a year.

Female West Highland White Terrier

hese West Highland
White Terrier puppies
have all the terrier
charm and vitality.

■ EXERCISE AND FEEDING
These dogs enjoy a regular walk
or sessions of play in the park but
won't be too upset if they miss a
day. (Keep a close eye on them
when out, as they are avid
hunters.) There are no special
feeding requirements.

Scottish Terrier

Size: male 10–11 in (25–28 cm)
female 9–10 in (23–25 cm)

Weight: male 19–23 lb (9–10 kg)
female 18–22 lb (8–10 kg)

■ ABOUT THIS BREED
Perhaps the best known, if not the oldest, of the Highland terriers, the modern Scottish Terrier hails from Aberdeen, where it was developed more than 100 years ago. The breed's correct standard was hotly debated in Britain until it was formalized in 1880.

This sturdy little dog has very short legs and the way it is groomed makes them look even shorter. Even so, it is a strong, active and surprisingly agile animal. The rough-textured, weather-resistant, broken coat comes in black, wheaten, or brindle of any color. The undercoat is short, dense and soft. Sharply pricked ears give the Scottish Terrier a thoughtful look.

■ TEMPERAMENT
Although somewhat dignified in its behavior, the Scottish Terrier makes a very good watchdog. It is inclined to be stubborn, however, and needs firm handling from an early age or it will try to dominate the entire household.

■ GROOMING
Regular brushing of the harsh wiry coat is important and extra care should be taken when the

Wheaten male
Scottish Terrier

...og is molting. Bathe or dry ...hampoo as necessary. The dog ...hould be professionally trimmed ...vice a year. The hair on the body ...e left long, like a skirt, while the ...air on the face is lightly trimmed ...nd brushed forward.

EXERCISE AND FEEDING
...iven a yard of reasonable size, ...he sporty Scottish Terrier will ...xercise itself, but it will happily ...ccompany you for a walk or play ...ession in the park. It delights in

Black male
Scottish
Terrier

fetching sticks and balls. No special feeding requirements, but beware of overfeeding or it will become obese and lazy.

SNAPSHOT

PERSONALITY **Happy, brave, loyal**
GROOMING **Regular brushing**
EXERCISE **Regular, moderate**
ENVIRONMENT **Ideal for apartment living, but likes to go wandering**
BE AWARE **Generally sturdy and robust, but prone to skin ailments, including sensitivity to fleas, which may cause chronic skin problems**

Border Terrier

Size: male 13–16 in (33–41 cm)
female 11–14 in (28–36 cm)

Weight: male 13–16 lb (6–7 kg)
female 11–14 lb (5–6 kg)

■ ABOUT THIS BREED

Once known as the Reedwater Terrier, the brave little Border Terrier evolved in the rugged border country between England and Scotland, sharing a common ancestry with other terriers. Perhaps the toughest of the terrier breeds, it was used to hunt foxes, otters and vermin.

One of the smallest of the working terriers, the Border Terrier has a wiry little body to go with its wiry double coat. It comes in reds, blue and tan, grizzle and tan, or wheaten. The muzzle and ears are usually dark and the undercoat very short and dense. The loose skin, which feels thick, enables the dog to wriggle into tight burrows. The head is somewhat different from that of other terriers and is often described as being like an otter's.

Grizzle and tan
male Border Terrier

TEMPERAMENT

Reliable and intelligent, Border Terriers are easily trained, obedient, sensible and bright. They are generally not aggressive with other dogs but may drive your cat crazy by hunting it. They love being part of a family and are unrestrained in their displays of affection, especially in greeting. They make good watchdogs.

GROOMING

The durable, wiry coat needs little grooming. Clip out any knots and brush occasionally with a bristle brush. The object is a completely natural look with no artifice.

Bathe only when necessary.

EXERCISE AND FEEDING

Border Terriers need plenty of exercise—they were bred to hunt and as plain, no-nonsense little working dogs, so they have great vitality and stamina. A bored Border Terrier can become destructive and chew things, so start gentle training from a very early age. There are no special feeding requirements.

Fox Terrier

Size: male 14–16 in (36–41 cm)
female 13–15 in (33–38 cm)

Weight: male 15–20 lb (7–9 kg)
female 13–18 lb (6–8 kg)

■ ABOUT THIS BREED

Fox Terriers are among the oldest of the terrier breeds and were bred to dig into burrows and catch small animals in their powerful jaws. They were also highly prized as ratters, more than earning their keep around stables. The Wire was bred for use in rough country, its coat being less vulnerable to damage than that of the Smooth. While the two types are remarkably similar and sometimes regarded as a single breed, they have been separate in the United States since 1984.

These popular, firm-bodied dogs are familiar to most people. The Smooth has a flat coat, while the Wire has a coarse, broken coat with a soft, short undercoat. Both come in mainly white, with tan, or black and tan markings. The feet are small and neat and the V-shaped ears fold and fall forward.

■ TEMPERAMENT

Keen, alert and independent, the Fox Terrier is a good watchdog, but needs to be firmly trained from an early age. It is quite reliable with children, but can be argumentative with other dogs, even large ones. Its high-pitched barking can be annoying and may cause problems with neighbors.

Tan and white male
Smooth Fox Terrier

GROOMING

Brush both types with a firm bristle brush, and bathe or dry shampoo only when necessary.

EXERCISE AND FEEDING

Unless you have a garden, these dogs need regular long walks or romps in the park, off the leash if possible. Keep on the leash in public places. No special feeding requirements, but watch the amount of food against the level of activity.

Tricolor female Wire Fox Terrier

Miniature Schnauzer

Size: male 12–14 in (30–36 cm)
female 11–13 in (28–33 cm)

Weight: male 11–18 lb (5–8 kg)
female 10–15 lb (5–7 kg)

■ ABOUT THIS BREED

This is the smallest of the three Schnauzer breeds (see p. 234), all of which originated in Germany. It is classified as a terrier only in the United States; most countries classify all three sizes of Schnauzer as utility or working dogs.

A strong, angular, square-looking dog, the Miniature Schnauzer has a harsh, wiry double coat that comes in salt and pepper or any solid color, sometimes with white on the chest. The thick, prominent eyebrows and long mustache are often trimmed to accentuate the dog's square-cut shape, and the tail is usually docked.

■ TEMPERAMENT

These dogs are noted for their reliability and affectionate nature and make excellent watchdogs. They are spirited and brave and, while not aggressive, they will take on much larger dogs should the need arise.

■ GROOMING

The wiry coat is reasonably easy to look after, but unless it is combed or brushed daily with a short wire brush, it will become

matted. Clip out any knots. The animal should be clipped all over to an even length twice a year, in spring and fall, but this is a job best left to an expert. Trim around the eyes and ears with blunt-nosed scissors and clean the whiskers after meals.

EXERCISE AND FEEDING

These energetic little dogs enjoy long, brisk, daily walks, and relish play sessions off the leash. No special feeding requirements.

Salt and pepper male
Miniature Schnauzers

SNAPSHOT

PERSONALITY Spirited, energetic, affectionate, lively
GROOMING Daily brushing
EXERCISE Regular, moderate
ENVIRONMENT Ideal for apartment living, but needs lots of exercise
BE AWARE Generally healthy, but may suffer from bladder stones, liver disease, skin disorders and cysts, known as "Schnauzer bumps"

Bull Terrier

Size: male 15–19 in (38–48 cm)
female 15–19 in (38–48 cm)

Weight: male 25–38 lb (11–17 kg)
female 25–38 lb (11–17 kg)

■ ABOUT THIS BREED

Bull Terriers were developed in Britain by crossing Bulldogs with Whippets and a variety of terriers. They were once used to bait bulls and for dog fighting, and were prized for their courage, tenacity, agility and speed. The Miniature was developed to have the same qualities in a slightly smaller dog.

A thick-set, muscular, well-proportioned animal, the Bull Terrier has a short, dense coat that comes in pure white, black, brindle, red, fawn and tricolor. Its most distinctive feature is its head, which is almost flat at the top, sloping evenly down to the end of the nose. The eyes are small, dark and closely set.

■ TEMPERAMENT

A tenacious fighter, the Bull Terrier is more of a danger to other dogs than to people. When firmly handled and properly trained, they are sweet natured, gentle and playful and make excellent watchdogs. Some dogs develop obsessive compulsive behaviors, such as tail chasing.

■ GROOMING

Brush the smooth, shorthaired coat with a firm bristle brush, and rub over with a piece of toweling.

White female
Standard Bull
Terrier

r chamois. Bathe
r dry shampoo
nly as necessary.
Wipe the eyes clean
wice a day. Check
etween the toes regularly.

■ EXERCISE AND FEEDING
ull Terriers need plenty of
xercise, but may be aggressive
vith other dogs. Keep them on a
ash at all times in public. No
pecial feeding requirements,
ut don't overfeed as they can
ecome obese and lazy.

The Miniature Bull Terrier is slightly
smaller than the Standard—both male
and female are up to 14 in (36 cm) tall
and up to 20 lb (9 kg) in weight. The
dog shown above is a black, brindle
and white male Miniature Bull Terrier.

SNAPSHOT
PERSONALITY **Determined, fearless**
GROOMING **Regular brushing**
EXERCISE **Regular, moderate**
ENVIRONMENT **Adapts well to urban living, but needs space to exercise and play**
BE AWARE **Some skin allergies and interdigital cysts. May suffer from a hereditary zinc deficiency that can be fatal. Some pups are born deaf**

Staffordshire Bull Terriers

English
Size: male 14–16 in (36–41 cm)
female 13–15 in (33–38 cm)

Weight: male 25–38 lb (11–17 kg)
female 23–35 lb (10–16 kg)

American
Size: male 17–19 in (43–48 cm)
female 16–18 in (41–46 cm)

Weight: male 40–50 lb (18–23 kg)
female 35–45 lb (16–20 kg)

■ ABOUT THESE BREEDS
A tough fighter, the Staffordshire
Bull Terrier was used to hunt
badgers in England and for bull
baiting and dog fighting until
these pastimes were outlawed.
Like the Bull Terrier, it has
Bulldog blood and a broad-
chested look of solidity. The
American version was developed
independently.

These well-proportioned,
muscular animals have short,
dense coats that come in white or
solid reds, fawn, brindle, black or
blue, with or without white.

■ TEMPERAMENT
Usually adored and adoring
within its own family circle, the

Brindle male
Staffordshire
Bull Terrier

Staffordshire needs firm and consistent training to curb its instinct to fight with other dogs. It makes an excellent watchdog. As pups, they tend to chew a lot so make sure you provide plenty of chew toys.

GROOMING

Brush the smooth, shorthaired coat every day with a firm bristle brush, and bathe or dry shampoo as needed. Rub over with a piece of toweling or chamois to make the coat gleam.

SNAPSHOT

PERSONALITY **Tough, reliable**
GROOMING **Daily brushing**
EXERCISE **Regular, moderate**
ENVIRONMENT **Adapts well to urban living, but needs firm handling and plenty of exercise**
BE AWARE **Relatively free of genetic problems, but may suffer from cataracts and have breathing problems. Can become overheated**

■ EXERCISE AND FEEDING
Staffordshire Bull Terriers must have plenty of regular exercise, but can be aggressive to other dogs. Keep on the leash in public places at all times. Don't overfeed.

Blue brindle female
American Staffordshire
Bull Terrier

Bedlington Terrier

Size: male 15–16 in (38–41 cm)
female 15–16 in (38–41 cm)

Weight: male 18–23 lb (8–10 kg)
female 18–23 lb (8–10 kg)

■ ABOUT THIS BREED
In full show trim, the Bedlington Terrier looks a bit like a lamb. Once known as the Rothbury Terrier, it gets its speed, agility and grace of movement from its Whippet blood. These attributes once made it popular with poachers, and it earned the nickname of Gypsy Dog. Its work also included ratting in the Northumberland mines.

The body is muscular and flexible, covered in a thick and slightly curly coat with a woolly undercoat. It comes in solid blue, liver and sandy beige, or parti-colored tan with any of these colors. The eyes are dark to light hazel, depending on coat color.

■ TEMPERAMENT
Although they can be stubborn, Bedlington Terriers are relatively easy to train and very affectionate.

They are enthusiastic diggers, love to be the center of attention and make very good watchdogs.

■ GROOMING
The coat does not shed and requires specialized clipping every six weeks, so it is probably

Blue male
Bedlington
Terrier

For showing, the ears are shaved closely, leaving a tassel on the tips.

SNAPSHOT

PERSONALITY **Intelligent, curious**
GROOMING **Specialized**
EXERCISE **Regular, moderate**
ENVIRONMENT **Adapts well to urban and apartment living, but needs plenty of exercise**
BE AWARE **Subject to serious inherited problems: a liver disorder (Copper Storage Disease), kidney disease and eye problems**

best if you can learn to do this yourself. The coat is thinned and clipped close to the head and body to accentuate body shape. Shave the ears closely, leaving a tassel on the tips. On the legs, the hair is left slightly longer. Have a professional groomer show you how to do it. Brush the dog regularly and clean and pluck inside the ears.

■ EXERCISE AND FEEDING
These active dogs need plenty of exercise and, like other terriers, will be bored and mischievous without it. They can be scrappy with other dogs and are fearsome fighters when provoked. No special feeding requirements.

Irish Terrier

Size: male 16–19 in (41–48 cm)
female 15–18 in (38–46 cm)

Weight: male 25–30 lb (11–14 kg)
female 23–28 lb (10–13 kg)

■ ABOUT THIS BREED
Known for its fighting spirit, the game little Irish Terrier is not for everyone, but it is very adaptable, courageous and loyal. Among the oldest of the terrier breeds, the Irish Terrier is only now regaining some of the immense popularity it once enjoyed. Admired for its pluck and unconquerable spirit, it was widely used as a guard dog and for hunting foxes, badgers and otters. Later, it excelled in the dog-fighting ring. It is closely related to the Wire Fox Terrier (see p. 156) but is slightly longer and larger.

The Irish Terrier looks a little like a smaller version of the Airedale Terrier (see p. 170). It has a hard, short and wiry coat that comes in solid red, yellow-red or red-wheaten.

■ TEMPERAMENT
While sociable with people and devoted to its owner, this dog has an often uncontrollable urge to fight with other dogs, which makes it quite unsuitable for inexperienced owners. It makes an excellent watchdog.

Red wheaten
female
Irish Terrier

Despite its reputation as a brave little fighter, the Irish Terrier is gentle and affectionate with its owner.

■ GROOMING

The hard double coat is easy to groom and rarely sheds. Brush regularly with a stiff bristle brush and remove the dead hair with a fine-toothed comb. Bathe only when necessary.

■ EXERCISE AND FEEDING

Being bred for active work, these dogs need plenty of regular exercise. When walking in public, always keep the dog firmly under control on a leash so that it is not able to fight with other dogs. No special feeding requirements.

Soft-coated Wheaten Terrier

Size: male 18–20 in (46–51 cm)
female 17–19 in (43–48 cm)

Weight: male 35–45 lb (16–20 kg)
female 30–40 lb (14–18 kg)

■ ABOUT THIS BREED
A jolly creature, the Soft-coated Wheaten Terrier seems to retain its carefree puppy ways into adulthood. Its enthusiasm and zest for life make it a delightful companion and pet. It is now rare in Ireland, where it is thought to have originated, as well as most other parts of the world. An exception is the United States, where it currently enjoys wide popularity. Like the Irish Terrier, it once earned its keep by performing guard duties, herding sheep and hunting badgers, otters, rats and rabbits.

This is a strong, medium-sized dog with good proportions and great stamina. The soft single coat is long and wavy and doesn't shed. It comes in wheaten shades (pale yellow to fawn). The tail is usually docked.

■ TEMPERAMENT
Friendly and appealing, the Wheaten Terrier is intelligent and easy to train. It makes an excellent watchdog.

Female
Soft-coated
Wheaten
Terrier

The face is adorned with a mustache and beard, and there is lots of hair falling over the eyes.

■ GROOMING

Frequent, even daily, combing of the long, profuse coat with a medium-toothed comb is recommended to keep it free of tangles. Start when the dog is a puppy, so that it becomes accustomed to this routine. The object is to achieve a natural look and brushing can make the soft coat fuzzy. Clean the eyes and check the ears carefully. Bathe or dry shampoo when necessary.

SNAPSHOT

PERSONALITY **Exuberant, friendly, intelligent, fearless**
GROOMING **Regular combing**
EXERCISE **Regular, moderate**
ENVIRONMENT **Adapts well to urban living, but dislikes boredom**
BE AWARE **Generally hardy, but may suffer from skin allergies, hip dysplasia, eye problems, such as PRA, and hereditary kidney disease**

■ EXERCISE AND FEEDING

These dogs can get by with moderate exercise as long as it is regular, and plenty of play to stop them from getting bored. No special feeding requirements.

Airedale Terrier

Size: male 23–24 in (58–61 cm)
female 22–23 in (56–58 cm)

Weight: male 40–50 lb (18–23 kg)
female 40–45 lb (18–20 kg)

■ ABOUT THIS BREED
A lively, water-loving dog,
the Airedale Terrier is very
adaptable and fits in well
with family life as long as it
has plenty of exercise and is not
allowed to rule the roost. The
largest of the terriers, it was
developed in Yorkshire to hunt
otters, badgers and wolves,
becoming especially popular in
the Aire Valley. It has since been
used extensively in police and
military work.

A medium-sized dog with a
strong, straight back, the Airedale
has a jaunty, alert stance. The
stiff, wiry, waterproof coat gave
protection against brambles. It
comes in a combination of dark
grizzle or black with red and tan
markings. The long, rather narrow
face is adorned with mustache,
beard and bushy eyebrows. The
eyes are small and dark. The nose

leather should be black. The
small, V-shaped ears fold forward
to the sides. The tail, usually
docked to the same height as the
head, is straight and carried erect

Black and
tan female
Airedale Terrier

TEMPERAMENT

Intelligent, reliable and loyal, Airedales make good watchdogs. They are not difficult to train, but don't respond well to harsh or overbearing training methods. They are naturally lively and love children.

■ GROOMING

The Airedale's hard, shorthaired, double coat is easy to groom and sheds very little. Brush regularly with a stiff bristle brush to remove the dead hair and bathe only when necessary.

■ EXERCISE AND FEEDING

Being bred for active work, these dogs need plenty of exercise. They are incorrigible diggers and are easily bored, so they need to be kept occupied. Extra oil can be included in the diet if your dog suffers from dry, itchy skin.

Sporting Dogs

SPORTING DOGS, also known as gundogs, were bred to work with hunters. Pointers were bred to sniff out game birds and, once located, to point toward them with an upraised leg. Setters also located game but would bend down out of the line of fire. The smaller, faster spaniels were bred to flush out game from the undergrowth for hunters to net or shoot; retrievers were bred to retrieve game once it was shot. Today, sporting dogs are popular pets. They retain their liveliness and love of exercise and are intensely loyal to their owners.

Cocker Spaniels

American
Size: male 13–16 in (33–41 cm)
female 12–15 in (30–38 cm)

Weight: male 25–35 lb (11–16 kg)
female 20–30 lb (9–14 kg)

English
Size: male 15–17 in (38–43 cm)
female 14–16 in (36–41 cm)

Weight: male 28–32 lb (13–15 kg)
female 26–30 lb (12–14 kg)

Cocker is named for its ability to flush woodcock from undergrowth. The slightly smaller American breed was recognized as separate in the 1930s.

This strong dog has a sturdy, compact body covered in silky, medium-length, flat-lying hair. The coat comes in solid reds, black, golden and liver, as well as particolors and tricolors with the color being broken up with white and occasional roans. Tails are usually docked short.

■ ABOUT THESE BREEDS
The spaniel family originated in Spain, as the name suggests, and various types became popular gundogs all over the world. The

Light blue roan male English Cocker Spaniel
Some one-color Cocker Spaniels display Rage Syndrome, unprovoked aggression, which is a occasionally reported i Springer Spaniels.

TEMPERAMENT

[En]ergetic, playful
[an]d responsive, the
[Co]cker Spaniel
[pe]rforms with
[en]dless enthusiasm,
[w]agging its stump of
[t]ail as well as its
[en]tire hindquarters
[fu]riously. It makes
[a] good watchdog.

Particolor female American Cocker
Spaniel. Some animals of this breed
have coats that reach the ground.

GROOMING

[Re]gular combing
[an]d brushing of
[th]e coat is
[im]portant. Bathe
[or] dry shampoo as
[ne]cessary. Check the
[ea]rs for grass seeds and
[si]gns of infection. Brush the hair
[on] the feet down over the toes
[an]d trim it level with the base
[of] the feet. Trim the hair around
[th]e pads, but not that between
[th]e toes.

EXERCISE AND FEEDING

[Th]ese dogs enjoy as much fun and
[ex]ercise as you can give them.
[Br]ush out burrs and tangles after
[th]e dog has been playing in grassy
[fie]lds or woods. Do not overfeed.

SNAPSHOT

PERSONALITY Joyful, affectionate
GROOMING Regular brushing
EXERCISE Moderate to vigorous
ENVIRONMENT Given plenty of
exercise, adapts well to urban life
BE AWARE Prone to genetic eye
problems and ear infections due
to poor ventilation of the
ear canals. The American
Cocker may also have
skin and spinal problems

Brittany

Size: male 18–21 in (46–53 cm)
female 18–20 in (46–51 cm)

Weight: male 30–45 lb (14–20 kg)
female 30–40 lb (14–18 kg)

■ ABOUT THIS BREED
The Brittany, or Breton, Spaniel has a long history in its native France, with records of these dogs going back for hundreds of years. Today, it has a growing following in the United States, where it was officially recognized as the Brittany in 1982. As well as being an excellent tracker and retriever, this dog is also a natural pointer, a trait possibly acquired through interbreeding with setters in the past. In the field, the Brittany tends to work close to its master. An agile and vigorous hunter, it is also admired for its grace and charming personality.

The smallest of the French spaniels, the Brittany is graceful, active and rugged, well muscled and has long-legged, elegant lines. The medium-length coat is dense and feathered on the ears, chest, underbody and upper parts of the legs. It comes in white with orange, black, brown or liver, as well as tricolors and roans. The tail is naturally short, but is still usually docked a little.

Orange and white
male Brittany

The Welsh Springer Spaniel (above) is sometimes mistaken for the Brittany in the field. However, it comes only in rich red and white, its coat is less wavy, and its leg feathering may be more profuse.

SNAPSHOT

PERSONALITY Friendly, energetic
GROOMING Regular brushing
EXERCISE Regular, vigorous
ENVIRONMENT Adapts well to urban living, but needs plenty of exercise and prefers outdoor life
BE AWARE Generally healthy, but prone to ear infections due to poor ventilation of ear canals, also genetic cataracts and PRA

■ TEMPERAMENT

Easy to train and handle, this loving and gentle animal is obedient and eager to please. It makes a good watchdog.

■ GROOMING

Regular brushing of the medium-length, flat coat is really all that is needed to keep it in good condition. Bathe or dry shampoo when necessary. Check the ears carefully for seeds and ticks, especially when the dog has been out in rough or brushy terrain.

■ EXERCISE AND FEEDING

These dogs love exercise and need vigorous activity to stay in peak condition. Do not overfeed.

English Springer Spaniel

Size: male 19–21 in (48–53 cm)
female 18–20 in (46–51 cm)

Weight: male 45–55 lb (20–25 kg)
female 40–50 lb (18–23 kg)

■ ABOUT THIS BREED

The handsome, robust English Springer Spaniel excels in the field at flushing out game, but also makes a delightful pet. It is a spirited and loyal companion. One of the largest of the spaniels, it is descended from the oldest spaniel stock and its blood probably runs in the veins of most modern spaniels. Once known as the Norfolk Spaniel, this all-weather retriever loves the water.

It is a strong dog with a sturdy, compact body. The soft, medium-length, flat-lying coat comes in all spaniel colors but mainly white with liver or black, with or without tan markings. It has large, heavy ears and, like other breeds with ears of a similar type, is prone to ear infections and other problems, such as picking up seeds. The tail is usually docked.

■ TEMPERAMENT

A quick learner, the Springer enjoys company, is patient with children and makes a good watchdog. Sadly, the breed is prone to an inherited behavioral disorder known as Rage Syndrome, which can cause

Liver and white
female English
Springer Spaniel

The long, heavy ears restrict free air circulation, so check them regularly.

aggression. Before buying a pup, check whether any of its relatives are afflicted by this condition.

■ GROOMING

The coat is fairly easy to maintain and regular brushing with a stiff bristle brush will keep it looking good. Take extra care when the animal is molting. Bathe or dry shampoo only when necessary but clean the ears regularly and check for signs of infection. Ask your vet about special cleaning aids.

■ EXERCISE AND FEEDING

The Springer enjoys as much exercise as you can give it. No special feeding requirements, but avoid overfeeding.

Golden Retriever

Size: male 22–24 in (56–61 cm)
female 20–22 in (51–56 cm)

Weight: male 60–80 lb (27–36 kg)
female 55–70 lb (25–32 kg)

■ ABOUT THIS BREED
The ancestry of the
breed is hard to prove,
but Golden Retrievers get
the seal of approval from
everyone who has ever owned
one. They share characteristics
with retrievers, Bloodhounds and
Water Spaniels, making them
very useful gundogs, renowned
for their tracking abilities. They
are thought to have been bred
in the United Kingdom by Lord
Tweedmouth, about 150 years ago.

This graceful and elegant dog
has a lustrous coat that comes in
any shade of gold or cream, with
the hair lying flat or gently waved
around the neck, shoulders and
hips. There is abundant feathering
on the underbody, legs and tail.

■ TEMPERAMENT
Well-mannered and intelligent,
these dogs have great charm. They

are easily trained, always patient
and are gentle with children.
They make great companions or
family pets. While unlikely to

ttack, Golden Retrievers make
ood watchdogs, loudly signaling
stranger's approach.

GROOMING

hese dogs shed a fair amount,
ut regular grooming will help.
he smooth, shorthaired double
oat is easy to groom. Comb and
rush with a firm bristle brush,
aying attention to the dense
ndercoat. Dry shampoo regularly,
ut bathe only when necessary.

■ EXERCISE AND FEEDING
Golden Retrievers like nothing
better than to work—if they have
regular strenuous duties, so
much the better. At the very
least they need a long daily
walk and preferably an
opportunity to run freely.
Encourage fetch games to help
your dog stay fit and trim.
Golden Retrievers love to swim
and should be allowed to do
so whenever possible. There
are no special feeding
requirements.

Male Golden Retriever

Labrador Retriever

Size: male 22–24 in (56–61 cm)
female 21–23 in (53–58 cm)

Weight: male 50–60 lb (23–27 kg)
female 45–55 lb (20–25 kg)

■ ABOUT THIS BREED
Courageous, loyal and
hard-working, the Labrador
Retriever has earned worldwide
respect for its dedication to duty.
Originally used by fishermen in
Newfoundland, rather than
Labrador as the name suggests,
these dogs became indispensable
as sled dogs, message-carriers and
general working dogs. Once
known as St John's Dogs, they
were part of every fishing crew.
They carry on this tradition of
service still, being widely used
as guide dogs for the blind and
in police work.

This strong, active dog with its
solid, powerful frame is a very
good swimmer. The tail, described
as an "otter" tail, is thick at the
base, round and tapered. The coat
is dense and waterproof with no
feathering, and comes in solid
black, yellow, fawn, cream, gold
or chocolate, occasionally with
white markings on the chest.

■ TEMPERAMENT
Reliable, obedient and easily
trained, Labradors are friendly,
good with children and make

PERSONALITY **Reliable, obedient, loving, loyal**
GROOMING **Regular brushing**
EXERCISE **Regular, vigorous**
ENVIRONMENT **Adapts well to urban living, but needs plenty of exercise and play**
BE AWARE **Prone to hip and elbow dysplasia. Also suffer from eye diseases, such as cataracts and PRA**

good watchdogs. They crave human attention and need to feel part of the family.

■ GROOMING

The smooth, shorthaired, double coat is easy to groom. Comb and brush regularly with a firm bristle brush, paying attention to the undercoat. Bathe or dry shampoo only when necessary.

■ EXERCISE AND FEEDING

These energetic dogs are delighted to work and play hard. No special feeding requirements, but don't overfeed as they can easily become obese and lazy.

Yellow male Labrador Retriever

Black male Labrador Retriever

German Pointers

Size: male 22–26 in (56–66 cm)
female 21–25 in (53–63 cm)

Weight: male 50–65 lb (23–29 kg)
female 45–60 lb (20–27 kg)

■ ABOUT THESE BREEDS
The ancestors of the German
Shorthaired Pointer include
Spanish and English Pointers,
the Bloodhound, French hounds
and Scandinavian breeds. In
search of perfection, they were
bred with terriers and Poodles.
The result was the German Wirehaired Pointer, with a tough,
rugged coat for good measure.

These superlative hunting dogs
have lean, muscular bodies and
powerful loins. The short, dense,
water-resistant coat of the
Shorthaired comes in solid black
or liver, or these colors with white
spots or flecks, or as roans. The
Wirehaired has a thick, wiry coat
of medium length, also water-
resistant. It comes in solid liver,
liver and white, and black and
white. The tails of both are
usually docked to half the length.

■ TEMPERAMENT
Intelligent and reasonably easy to
train, the German Pointer has a
mind of its own and should never
be allowed to get the upper hand.

Liver and white
male German
Shorthaired Pointer

GROOMING

Brush the smooth coat of the Shorthaired regularly with a firm bristle brush. A rub with a piece of toweling or chamois will leave the coat gleaming. The short, wiry coat of the Wirehaired needs a little more attention. Brush it about twice a week with a firm bristle brush and thin it in spring and fall. Bathe only when necessary.

■ EXERCISE AND FEEDING

These dogs need plenty of vigorous exercise. No special feeding requirements, but match the amount of food with the dog's level of activity.

Liver roan male German Wirehaired Pointer. These dogs may be easier to train and less bouncy than their Shorthaired counterparts.

SNAPSHOT

PERSONALITY **Intelligent, reliable, keen; the Wirehaired can be slightly aggressive to other dogs**
GROOMING **Regular brushing**
EXERCISE **Regular, vigorous**
ENVIRONMENT **Adapts to urban living, but needs plenty of space**
BE AWARE **Generally hardy and long-lived, but prone to ear infections. Some genetic problems**

Chesapeake Bay Retriever

Size: male 23–26 in (58–66 cm)
female 21–24 in (53–61 cm)

Weight: male 60–75 lb (27–34 kg)
female 55–65 lb (25–29 kg)

■ ABOUT THIS BREED
The Chesapeake Bay Retriever was developed entirely in the United States, in the Maryland area, from a pair of shipwrecked puppies that were crossed with various dogs used as retrievers. The result was an intrepid dog, highly valued for its prowess and extraordinary ability to remember where each bird falls and retrieve them all efficiently.

Although not universally considered handsome, this medium-sized dog is athletic and strong. The coat is tight, dense, wavy and totally water-resistant; the soft undercoat is quite oily and the feet are webbed. It is a strong swimmer and can swim even in heavy, icy seas. Water is shed completely with a quick shake, so the dog stays warm and dry. The coat color varies from dark tan to dark brown, the colors of dead grass, so it is well camouflaged for its work.

■ TEMPERAMENT
These dogs are courageous and intelligent, but they are also

Dark tan male
Chesapeake
Bay Retriever

strong, and require patience to train. They have a tendency to be territorial and aggressive with other dogs so they need firm handling and good management. They make good watchdogs.

GROOMING
The dense, harsh, shorthaired coat is easy to groom. Brush with a firm bristle brush and bathe only if necessary. Bathing destroys the natural waterproofing of the coat.

■ EXERCISE AND FEEDING
These dogs need a great deal of vigorous activity, including swimming, to stay in peak condition. There are no special feeding requirements but measure the quantity of food given against the dog's level of activity.

SNAPSHOT

PERSONALITY **Keen worker, but can be aggressive with other dogs**
GROOMING **Regular brushing**
EXERCISE **Vigorous; loves to swim**
ENVIRONMENT **Adapts to urban living, but is best in the country**
BE AWARE **While this breed is generally very healthy, some dogs may suffer from hip dysplasia and hereditary eye diseases**

Vizsla

Size: male 22–26 in (56–66 cm)
female 20–24 in (51–61 cm)

Weight: male 45–60 lb (20–27 kg)
female 40–55 lb (18–25 kg)

■ ABOUT THIS BREED

Hungary's national dog, the agile Vizsla was little known elsewhere until after World War II. This excellent tracker, now becoming increasingly popular outside its country of origin, is also known as the Hungarian Pointer. The Vizsla was bred for hunting, pointing and retrieving. It is possible that it is descended from the Turkish Yellow Dog and the Transylvanian Hound, but it is more likely to be the result of crosses with the Weimaraner. A good swimmer, it originally worked the plains, woodlands and marshes, working just as well on land as in water.

This handsome, lean, well-muscled dog moves gracefully either at a lively trotting gait or in a swift, ground-covering gallop. The coat is short and close, rusty gold to sandy yellow in color and greasy to the touch.

■ TEMPERAMENT

Although good natured, intelligent and easy to train, the Vizsla is somewhat sensitive and

...eeds to be handled gently. It is
...eliable with children, quickly
...dapts to family life and makes
... good watchdog.

■ GROOMING
...he smooth, shorthaired
...oat is easy to keep in peak
...ondition. Brush with a firm
...ristle brush, and dry shampoo
...ccasionally. Bathe with mild
...oap only when necessary. The
...ails should be kept trimmed.

■ EXERCISE AND FEEDING
Vizslas are great jumpers and, if
bored, will escape from any yard
that does not have a sufficiently
high fence. They are energetic
working dogs with enormous
stamina, and need plenty of
opportunity to run, preferably off
the leash, as well as a lot of
regular exercise. If these dogs are
allowed to get bored, they can
become destructive. There are no
special feeding requirements.

...usty gold male Vizsla

Weimaraner

Size: male 24–27 in (61–69 cm)
female 22–25 in (56–63 cm)

Weight: male 55–70 lb (25–32 kg)
female 50–65 lb (23–29 kg)

■ ABOUT THIS BREED
Once widely used in
Germany to hunt large prey,
such as bears and wild pigs,
the Weimaraner became prized in
more recent times as a gundog
and retriever of small game, such
as waterfowl. It is sometimes
referred to as the silver ghost.

This superb hunting dog has a
well-proportioned, athletic body.
The sleek, close-fitting coat comes
in silver-gray to mouse shades,
often lighter on the head and ears.
The striking eyes are blue-gray or
amber. The tail is usually docked.

■ TEMPERAMENT
Alert, intelligent and strong-
willed, the Weimaraner is a
versatile breed that is happiest
when it is fully occupied with
work or tasks that engage its
mind. It requires firm handling by
a strong adult, and thorough
training. It is good with children
and makes an excellent watchdog

GROOMING

he smooth, shorthaired coat is
asy to keep in peak condition.
rush with a firm bristle brush,
d dry shampoo occasionally.
athe with mild soap only when
ecessary. A rub over with a
amois will make the coat

gleam. Inspect feet and mouth
for damage after exercise or
work sessions. Keep nails
trimmed, and protect the nose
from summer sun.

■ EXERCISE AND FEEDING
These are powerful working
dogs with great stamina.
They love to retrieve and
need opportunities to run
free. As they are prone
to bloat, it is better to
feed them two or
three small meals a
day, preferably after
exercise, rather than
give one large meal.

ver-gray male Weimaraner

Irish Setter

Size: male 25–27 in (63–69 cm)
female 23–25 in (58–63 cm)

Weight: male 55–65 lb (25–29 kg)
female 50–60 lb (23–27 kg)

■ ABOUT THIS BREED

The Irish Setter, also known as
the Red Setter, evolved in the
British Isles over the past 200
years from a variety of setters,
spaniels and pointers. It is a little
lighter and speedier than other
setters, having been bred to cope
with Ireland's marshy terrain. Like
all setters, these dogs were bred to
"set," or locate, game birds and
then to remain still while the
hunter shot or netted the birds.

The Irish Setter's profusely
feathered silky coat comes in rich
shades of chestnut to mahogany,
sometimes with splashes of white
on the chest and feet. The ears are
long and low-set and the legs are
long and muscular.

■ TEMPERAMENT

Like most sporting dogs, Irish
Setters are full of energy and high
spirits. They can also be very

affectionate, sometimes over-
whelmingly so. Being easily

Mahogany male
Irish Setter

istracted, they can be difficult to
ᵓain, but the effort will be
ᵓewarding for both owner and
ᵓog. Training must be consistent,
ᵓut never harsh. Not very good as
ᵓ watchdog.

GROOMING

ᵓaily combing and brushing of
ᵓe soft, flat, medium-length coat
is all that is required to keep it in
excellent condition. Keep it free
of burrs and tangles, and give a
little extra care when the dog is
molting. Bathe or dry shampoo
only when necessary.

■ EXERCISE AND FEEDING

Setters need plenty of exercise, if
possible, running free. If they don't
get a long, brisk walk at least once
a day, they will be restless and
difficult to manage. Feed two or
three small meals, after exercise,
rather than one large meal a day.

SNAPSHOT

PERSONALITY Lively, affectionate
GROOMING Daily combing
EXERCISE Regular, extensive and
vigorous exercise is essential
ENVIRONMENT Needs plenty of
space to run free. Unsuited to
apartment living
BE AWARE Prone to epilepsy
and severe skin allergies.
Also bloat, and genetic
eye and joint problems

Other Setters

Gordon
Size: male 25–28 in (63–71 cm)
female 23–26 in (58–66 cm)

Weight: male 60–70 lb (27–32 kg)
female 55–65 lb (25–29 kg)

English
Size: male 25–27 in (63–69 cm)
female 24–26 in (61–66 cm)

Weight: male 60–66 lb (27–30 kg)
female 55–62 lb (25–28 kg)

■ ABOUT THESE BREEDS
The Gordon Setter, the only
Scottish setter, has great stamina.
The silky coat is generously

feathered and is always a
gleaming black with tan to
reddish mahogany markings. On
the face, the markings are clearly
defined and include a spot over
each eye. The elegant English
Setter has a finely chiseled head
and large nostrils. Its flat, straight
coat is of medium length and
comes in white, flecked with
combinations of black, lemon,
liver, and black and tan. There is
feathering along the underbody
and on the ears.

Black and tan male
Gordon Setter

TEMPERAMENT

Calmer than other setters and more reserved with strangers, the Gordon Setter is an excellent, affectionate companion. The gentle and high-spirited English Setter takes its duties seriously, and when one becomes part of a family, it is quiet and very loyal.

GROOMING

Regular combing and brushing of either soft, flat, medium-length coat is all that is required to keep it in excellent condition. It is important to check for burrs and tangles, and to give extra care when the dog is molting. Bathe or dry shampoo only when necessary. Trim the hair on the bottom of the feet and clip the nails.

Orange belton (spotted) male English Setter

EXERCISE AND FEEDING

If these dogs don't have a long daily walk, they will be restless. Feed two or three small meals a day rather than one large one.

Hounds

DOGS FROM THIS GROUP are among the most ancient breeds. The first hunting dogs for which there are historical records were Greyhounds. Developed to chase and kill large prey, many hounds have great stamina and speed. They are roughly divided into sighthounds and scenthounds, depending on how they locate their prey. Some scenthounds are not especially fast, choosing instead to corner their prey. These days, hounds are often used for racing or in police work. They make good pets but need a lot of exercise.

Beagle

Size: male 14–16 in (36–41 cm)
female 13–15 in (33–38 cm)

Weight: male 22–25 lb (10–11 kg)
female 20–23 lb (9–10 kg)

Beagles bay when they bark and they are also rather inclined to wander.

■ ABOUT THIS BREED
Packs of Beagles were
traditionally used to follow the
scent of hares, which they did
enthusiastically. The name
may come from the
Celtic word for small,
beag, or the French for
gape throat, *begueule*.

The modern dog is
considerably larger than those
of earlier times, which were often
carried in pockets or saddlebags.

This muscular little dog is the
smallest of the pack hounds. Its
dense waterproof coat comes in
combinations of white, black, tan,
red, lemon and blue mottle.

■ TEMPERAMENT
Beagles need firm handling as
they are strong willed and not
always easy to train. When they
pick up an interesting smell, it

Tricolor male
Beagle

s sometimes hard to get their attention. They are alert and even-tempered, rarely aggressive and love children. Indeed, they crave companionship. They do not make particularly good watchdogs.

GROOMING
The Beagle's smooth, shorthaired coat is easy to look after. Brush with a firm bristle brush, and dry shampoo occasionally. Bathe with mild soap only when necessary. Be sure to check the floppy ears carefully for signs of infection and keep the toenails trimmed.

■ EXERCISE AND FEEDING
Energetic and with great stamina, the Beagle needs plenty of exercise, but a yard of reasonable size will take care of most of its needs. A brisk daily walk will cover the rest. No special feeding requirements, but if you use food as a training motivator, be careful that the dog does not become obese and lazy.

SNAPSHOT

PERSONALITY Energetic, alert, joyful, even-tempered
GROOMING Regular brushing
EXERCISE Regular, moderate
ENVIRONMENT Adapts well to urban living, but likes to run free
BE AWARE May suffer from spinal problems, epilepsy, skin conditions and genetic eye diseases, such as glaucoma and cataracts

Dachshund

Standard
Size: male about 8 in (20 cm)
female about 8 in (20 cm)

Weight: male 20–22 lb (9–10 kg)
female 18–20 lb (8–9 kg)

Miniature
Size: male about 6 in (15 cm)
female about 6 in (15 cm)

Weight: male up to 11 lb (5 kg)
female up to 11 lb (5 kg)

■ ABOUT THIS BREED
These extraordinary "sausage" dogs come in a range of colors, sizes and coat types—it seems there's a sturdy little Dachshund for every taste, although most owners have decided preferences.

The Dachshund (pronounced dak sund) originated in Germany many hundreds of years ago—*Dachs* is the German word for badger. The Dachshund was bred to hunt and follow its prey to earth, gradually becoming highly evolved, with shortened legs to dig prey animals out and go down inside the burrows. Smaller Dachshunds were bred to hunt rabbits and stoats.

Dachshunds have many "terrier" characteristics. They are versatile and courageous dogs and have been known to take on foxes and otters as well as badgers.

Dachshunds come in two sizes—Standard and Miniature. All Dachshunds have low-slung, muscular, elongated bodies with very short legs and the strong forequarters developed for

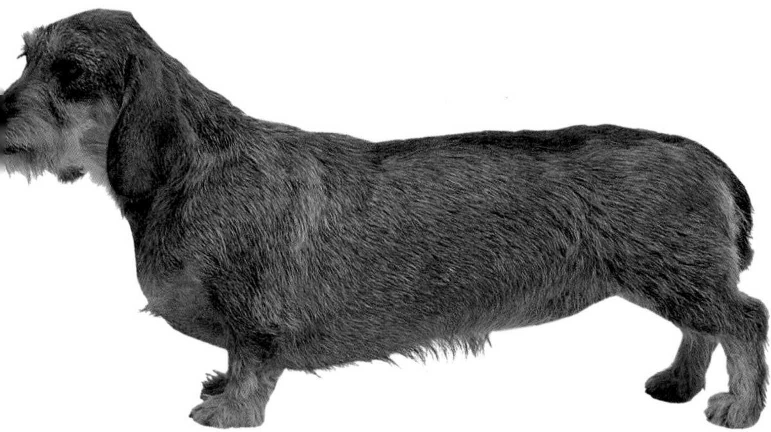

Brindle female Standard
Wirehaired Dachshund

igging. The skin is loose and the
oat comes in three distinct types:
mooth, short and dense;
onghaired, soft, flat and straight
ith feathering; and wirehaired,
ith a short double coat, a beard
nd bushy eyebrows.

The wirehaired is the least
ommon and was developed to
unt in brushy thickets. The
hree coat types come in a range
of solid colors, two-colored,
brindled, tiger-marked or
dappled. These dogs have
a big bark for their size,
which will warn you
of visitors and might
deter intruders.

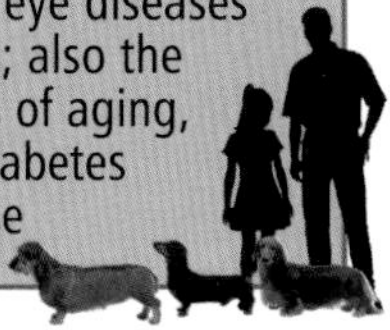

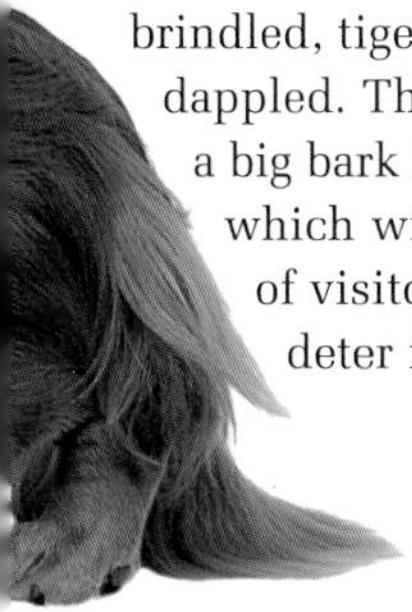

Shaded red female Standard
Longhaired Dachshund

These dogs are enthusiastic diggers and will wreak havoc in a garden. As they are a rather long-lived breed, Dachshunds suffer from problems common to aging dogs, such as obesity, diabetes and cardiac disease. They are also subject to genetic eye diseases and skin problems, including pattern baldness on the ears. Herniated disks in the back can cause severe pain and paralysis of the hind legs.

■ TEMPERAMENT

Alert, lively and affectionate, Dachshunds are great little characters, good company and reasonably obedient when carefully trained. They can be slightly aggressive to strangers but make wonderful house pets. Miniatures are perhaps less suited to households in which there are very young children, as they are quite vulnerable to injury from rough handling.

Red male Standard
Smooth Dachshund

Black and tan male Miniature
Smooth Dachshund

GROOMING

Regular brushing with a bristle brush is appropriate for all coat types. Dry shampoo or bathe when necessary, but always make sure the dog is thoroughly dry and warm after a bath. The smooth variety will come up gleaming if you rub it with a piece of toweling or a chamois. Check the ears regularly.

■ EXERCISE AND FEEDING

These are active dogs with surprising stamina and they love a regular walk or session of play in the park. Be careful, however, when pedestrians are about as Dachshunds are more likely to be stepped on than more visible dogs. They should be discouraged from jumping as they are prone to spinal damage.

There are no special feeding requirements, but don't overfeed, as Dachshunds have a tendency to become overweight and lazy. This can constitute a serious health risk, by putting added strain on the spine and spinal disks.

Basset Hound

Size: male 12–15 in (30–38 cm)
female 11–14 in (28–36 cm)

Weight: male 50–65 lb (23–29 kg)
female 45–60 lb (20–27 kg)

■ ABOUT THIS BREED

While most Basset breeds originated in France (*bas* means "low" in French), the Basset Hound was developed in Britain only about 100 years ago. Its ability to concentrate on a particular scent quickly earned it respect as a hunting partner (but be aware that when it is focused on an interesting smell, it can sometimes be hard to get the dog's attention).

This sturdy dog has short, stocky legs on which the skin is loose and folded. Much of the dog's weight is concentrated at the front of the long, barrel-shaped body. The shorthaired coat sheds only moderately and comes in combinations of white with tan, black and, occasionally, lemon. The ears are long and velvety.

■ TEMPERAMENT

The mournful face of this gentle, lovable hound belies its lively personality. Good-natured and sociable, it is gentle with children and fits into family life well. With proper training, it will be obedient but it is not a good watchdog.

GROOMING

The smooth, shorthaired coat is easy to groom. Comb and brush with a firm bristle brush, and shampoo only when necessary. Wipe under the ears every week and trim toenails regularly.

EXERCISE AND FEEDING

Plenty of moderate exercise will help to keep the Basset Hound healthy and happy, but discourage it from jumping and stressing the front legs. Do not allow it to overeat because extra weight places too great a load on the legs and spine. As the breed is prone to bloat, it is also wise to feed two or three small meals a day instead of one large meal.

SNAPSHOT

PERSONALITY Gentle and loyal
GROOMING Weekly brushing, paying attention to ears and feet
EXERCISE Regular, moderate
ENVIRONMENT Well suited to urban living
BE AWARE Because the ears are long and heavy, they are susceptible to infection. These dogs also suffer from bloat and skin infections

Liver and white male
Basset Hound

Basenji

Size: male 16–17 in (41–43 cm)
female 15–16 in (38–41 cm)

Weight: male 25–35 lb (11–16 kg)
female 20–30 lb (9–14 kg)

■ ABOUT THIS BREED
Although these handsome dogs are well known for being barkless, they are not silent, and "yodel" when happy. This ancient breed originated in Africa, where they were used for hunting and valued for their great stamina. They were introduced into Europe and then North America in the twentieth century.

The Basenji is a compact, muscular, medium-sized dog, with a distinctive trotting gait. Its loose, silky, shorthaired coat comes in combinations of white, tan, chestnut, brindle and black. When alert, the forehead is creased with wrinkles, giving the dog a worried look. The tail is tightly curled over the back and the small pointed ears are set well forward. The breeding pattern is unusual, with the bitch coming into season only once a year.

an and white
emale Basenji

■ TEMPERAMENT

Alert, affectionate, energetic and curious, the Basenji loves to play and makes a good pet, as long as it is handled regularly from an early age. Although it is very intelligent it needs firm and consistent training and is not a particularly good watchdog.

■ GROOMING

The Basenji is as fastidious as a cat about its personal grooming, even washing itself with its paws. The smooth, shorthaired, silky coat needs minimal care. Comb and brush with a firm bristle brush, and shampoo only when really necessary.

■ EXERCISE AND FEEDING

Vigorous daily exercise will keep the Basenji trim and fit—they have a tendency to become fat and lazy unless the owner is conscientious about exercise. Basenjis like to chew, so provide them with plenty of toys that they can destroy. They also like to climb, and can easily negotiate chain-wire fences. Some green vegetables should be included in its food to mimic the natural diet.

Whippet

Size: male 18–20 in (46–51 cm)
female 17–19 in (43–48 cm)

Weight: male 20–22 lb (9–10 kg)
female 19–21 lb (9–10 kg)

Brindle (left) and
particolor female
Whippets

■ ABOUT THIS BREED
Gentle, affectionate and
adaptable, the Whippet makes a
delightful companion and jogging
partner. It is descended from
the Greyhound, perhaps with
some terrier blood, and was
used for hunting rabbits in
northern England.

It was also pitted against its
peers in a pastime known as rag
racing. When given the signal
with a handkerchief, competing
dogs would streak toward their
owners from a standing start. The
Whippet's lean, fine-boned and
delicate appearance belies its
strength and speed—it can
accelerate rapidly to about
35 mph (55 km/h).

The muzzle is long and slender
and the overall impression is one
of streamlined elegance. The fine,
dense coat comes in many colors
or in combinations of colors.

Particolor
female
Whippet

TEMPERAMENT

Gentle and sensitive, the Whippet makes a surprisingly docile and obedient pet, although it is inclined to be nervous and must be handled gently. It is not the best choice if there are lively children in the family, but it is clean and well behaved in the house, and settles happily into the family routine. It is not a very good watchdog. While it is easily trained, its owners must take great care not to break its spirit by being harsh or overbearing.

GROOMING

The smooth, fine, shorthaired coat is easy to groom. Brush with a firm bristle brush, and bathe only when necessary. A rub all over with a chamois will make the coat gleam. Keep the toenails clipped.

EXERCISE AND FEEDING

Whippets kept as pets should have regular opportunities to run free on open ground as well as have long, brisk, daily walks on the leash. There are no special feeding requirements, but avoid food that is too starchy.

SNAPSHOT

PERSONALITY Sensitive, gentle, highly strung
GROOMING Regular brushing
EXERCISE Regular, moderate
ENVIRONMENT Adapts well to urban living, but needs plenty of space for exercise
BE AWARE Sensitive to cold and sunburn; also subject to genetic eye diseases, such as cataracts and PRA

Norwegian Elkhound

Size: male 19–21 in (48–53 cm)
female 18–20 in (46–51 cm)

Weight: male 45–55 lb (20–25 kg)
female 40–50 lb (18–23 kg)

■ ABOUT THIS BREED

Dogs of this kind have been used to hunt bears, elk and moose since Viking times. They would chase and hold the prey until hunters arrived for the kill. They were also used to pull sleds.

Although it is totally silent while tracking, the Elkhound is perhaps the most "talkative" dog of all. It has a whole vocabulary of sounds, each with a different meaning, and you will soon learn to recognize its way of telling you there are strangers about.

A member of the Spitz family, the Elkhound has a short, thickset body with the tail tightly curled over the back. The coat comes in various shades of gray, with black tips on the outer coat, and lighter hair on the chest, underbody, legs and underside of the tail. There is a thick ruff around the neck.

■ TEMPERAMENT

While gentle and devoted to its owner, the Elkhound needs consistent training that is firm but never harsh. Although adaptable, it likes a set routine.

Gray and black male
Norwegian Elkhound

The handsome Norwegian Elkhound can adapt to warmer climates than its homeland as the thick coat insulates it from both heat and cold.

■ GROOMING

Regular brushing of the hard, coarse, weatherproof coat is important, with extra care when the dog is molting its dense undercoat. At this time, the dead hair clings to the new hair and must be removed with a rubber brush designed for the task. Bathing is largely unnecessary.

■ EXERCISE AND FEEDING

Bred for hard work, the agile and energetic Norwegian Elkhound revels in strenuous activity. The more space it has to move around the better. There are no special feeding requirements, but don't overfeed—it is a thrifty feeder and tends to gain weight quickly.

Saluki

Size: male 23–28 in (58–71 cm)
female 20–27 in (51–69 cm)

Weight: male 40–60 lb (18–27 kg)
female 35–55 lb (16–25 kg)

■ ABOUT THIS BREED

The athletic appearance of the Saluki is one of total grace and symmetry. Slim and fine-boned, it is built for speed and capable of bursts of 40 mph (65 km/h) or more, but it also has exceptional endurance. The galloping gait is unusual and unique to sighthounds, with all four feet being off the ground at the same time when the animal is in full chase. This gives the impression that the dog is flying.

There are two types of coat, smoothhaired and feathered. Both have feathering on the ears and on the long, curved tail, but the smooth variety has none on the legs. The soft, smooth, silky coat comes in black and tan, white, cream, fawn, gold and red, as well as various combinations of these. A dog with a small patch of white in the middle of its forehead is thought by Bedouin tribes to have "the kiss of Allah" and is seen as special. The aristocratic head is narrow and well proportioned and the feathered ears are long and hanging.

Gold male Saluki. The fast and agile Saluki makes an excellent jogging companion, but be aware that it can jump very high fences.

TEMPERAMENT

Gentle, affectionate and intensely loyal, Salukis quickly become part of the family, although they may remain aloof with strangers. They are not at all aggressive but can be rather sensitive and, while easy to train, they become nervous and timid if the trainer's manner is overbearing or harsh.

SNAPSHOT

PERSONALITY **Gentle, sensitive, loyal and affectionate**
GROOMING **Daily brushing**
EXERCISE **Regular, moderate**
ENVIRONMENT **Adapts to urban living if given adequate exercise**
BE AWARE **Prone to cancer and genetic eye diseases, such as cataracts and PRA. Apply sunscreen regularly to noses of pale/mottled dogs**

■ GROOMING

Comb and brush the soft, smooth, silky coat with a firm bristle brush, and shampoo only when necessary. Be careful not to overbrush as this may break the coat. There is little shedding. Trim the hair between the toes to avoid matting and sore feet.

■ EXERCISE AND FEEDING

As well as long daily walks, Salukis should have regular opportunities to run free on open ground. There are no special feeding requirements, but they tend to be light eaters. They also drink less than other dogs.

Bloodhound

Size: male 25–27 in (63–69 cm)
female 23–25 in (58–63 cm)

Weight: male 90–110 lb (40–50 kg)
female 80–100 lb (36–45 kg)

■ ABOUT THIS BREED
Brought to England by
William the Conqueror,
the solemn-looking
Bloodhound, also known
as the Flemish Hound,
can trace its ancestry
directly to eighth-century
Belgium. It has entered
legend and literature as the
archetypal sleuth dog with the
mournful howl, but it never kills
its prey. It is able to follow any
scent, even a human's, which is
a rare ability among dogs.

Large and powerful, the
Bloodhound looks tougher than
it really is. The skin is loose and
seems several sizes too large for
the body. The coat is short and
dense, fine on the head and ears,
and comes in tan with black or
liver, tawny, or solid red. There
is sometimes a little white on the
chest, feet and the tip of the tail.

■ TEMPERAMENT
Sensitive and gentle, the Bloodhound becomes devoted to its
master, and gets along well with

Black and
tan female
Bloodhound

…eople and other dogs. It is rarely …icious, but is too shy to be a very …ood watchdog.

◀ GROOMING

…he smooth, shorthaired coat is …asy to groom. Brush with a firm …ristle brush, and bathe only

when necessary. A rub with a rough towel or chamois will leave the coat gleaming. Clean the long, floppy ears regularly. A well-padded bed is recommended to avoid calluses on the joints.

■ EXERCISE AND FEEDING
A Bloodhound loves a good run and needs a lot of exercise, but if it picks up an interesting scent you may have difficulty in getting its attention. No special feeding needs, but as this breed is prone to bloat, it's best to feed two or three small meals a day instead of one large one. Avoid exercise after meals.

Rhodesian Ridgeback

Size: male 25–27 in (63–69 cm)
female 24–26 in (61–66 cm)

Weight: male 75–85 lb (34–38 kg)
female 70–80 lb (32–36 kg)

■ ABOUT THIS BREED
Although these dogs
originated in South
Africa, it was in what
is now known as
Zimbabwe that they were prized
for their ability to hunt lion and
other large game.

This strong, active dog has a
dense, glossy coat that comes in
solid shades of light wheaten to
red with a dark muzzle and sometimes a little white on the chest.
When alert, the brow is wrinkled.

■ TEMPERAMENT
Like many powerful dogs, the
Rhodesian Ridgeback is a gentle,
friendly animal, although it can
be a tenacious fighter when
aroused. It makes an outstanding
watchdog and a devoted family
pet. Intelligent and good natured,
it is easy to train, but should be
treated gently so as not to break
its spirit or make it aggressive.
Training should start while the
dog is still young enough and
small enough to manage.

■ GROOMING
The smooth, shorthaired
coat is easy to
groom.

The breed gets its name from a peculiarity of the coat—a well-defined dagger-shaped ridge of hair that lies along the spine and grows in the opposite direction to the rest of the coat.

Brush with a firm bristle brush, and shampoo only when necessary.

■ EXERCISE AND FEEDING

These dogs have great stamina and you will tire long before they do, but they will adapt to your exercise regimen. They love to swim. No special feeding needs, but beware of overfeeding— they will eat all they can get and still act hungry.

Wheaten male
Rhodesian Ridgeback

Afghan Hound

Size: male 27–29 in (69–74 cm)
female 25–27 in (63–69 cm)

Weight: male 55–65 lb (25–29 kg)
female 50–60 lb (23–27 kg)

■ ABOUT THIS BREED
While undeniably elegant and,
when in peak condition, a thing
of beauty, the Afghan Hound is
not an easy-care pet. Choose one
only if you are prepared to make
a big commitment in time, or use
a professional groomer.

A hardy breed, agile and with
great stamina, the Afghan Hound
has been used for many centuries
in its native land to hunt gazelle
and other large prey, including
snow leopards. It was especially
favored by royalty.

The coat is very long, straight
and silky, except on the face and
along the spine, and comes in all
colors and some combinations.
White markings are not liked by
breed fanciers. Thick falls of hair
on the legs protect the animal
from cold. The end of the tail
should curl in a complete ring.
The gait is free and springy.

Chocolate
brindle male
Afghan Hound

■ TEMPERAMENT

The enormous popularity of these dogs during the 1970s meant that many were acquired for the wrong reasons. Although they are intelligent, Afghan Hounds are not easy to train and, being quite large, they are not easy to handle, either. They are definitely not a fashion accessory, and owners need to establish a genuine relationship with them. Too many of these striking dogs have been abandoned because their owners had unrealistic expectations. They are not good watchdogs.

■ GROOMING

The long, thick coat demands a great deal of attention and must be brushed every day. Anti-tangle conditioners may help. Dry shampoo when necessary and bathe once a month.

■ EXERCISE AND FEEDING

These dogs love open spaces and must be allowed to run free as well as have long daily walks. No special feeding requirements.

Borzoi

Size: male at least 29 in (74 cm)
female at least 27 in (69 cm)

Weight: male 70–90 lb (32–41 kg)
female 65–85 lb (29–38 kg)

■ ABOUT THIS BREED
The well-mannered Borzoi, also known as the Russian Wolfhound, is a dog of grace and beauty, dignified and gentle. If you want a constant companion and can give it the exercise and love it craves, this may be the dog for you. Borzois were used in pairs by members of the Russian aristocracy to chase wolves. The prey was caught and held by the dogs until the mounted hunter arrived for the kill. They are probably descended from the "gaze hounds" of the Middle East, which they resemble.

A tall, elegant, deep-chested dog, the Borzoi's lean, muscular body is designed for speed. The long, silky, often wavy coat is profusely feathered, and comes in all colors, usually white with colored markings. The small ears are pointed and well feathered.

■ TEMPERAMENT
Gentle, reserved and sometimes nervous around children, Borzois are affectionate with their owners

...nd tolerant of other dogs, but ...hey need plenty of attention. ...hey are not good watchdogs.

GROOMING

...rush the long, silky coat ...egularly with a firm bristle ...rush, and dry shampoo when ...ecessary. Bathing presents a

Blue sable male Borzoi

SNAPSHOT

PERSONALITY Gentle, reserved, sensitive, affectionate
GROOMING Regular brushing
EXERCISE Regular, moderate
ENVIRONMENT Adapts well to urban living, but needs plenty of exercise and space to run free
BE AWARE Prone to bloat. As they age, they may also be susceptible to PRA and cataracts

problem with such a tall dog but shouldn't be needed very often. Clip the hair between the toes to keep the feet comfortable and to stop them from spreading. Borzois need a well-padded bed to prevent calluses and irritation to elbows.

■ EXERCISE AND FEEDING
To maintain their fitness these dogs need plenty of exercise, including regular opportunities to run off the leash. It's a good idea to feed small meals two or three times a day as they are susceptible to bloat. Avoid exercise after meals.

Greyhound

Size: male 28–30 in (71–76 cm)
female 27–28 in (68–71 cm)

Weight: male 55–70 lb (25–32 kg)
female 50–65 lb (23–29 kg)

■ ABOUT THIS BREED

Agile and fleet of foot, this breed
is one of the oldest known, long
valued for its hunting prowess. Its
elegant lines are often depicted on
royal coats of arms. Greyhounds
probably originated in the Middle
East but they also have a long
history in Europe. They were
much sought after as hunting
dogs—peasants were not allowed
to own them because of their
usefulness in poaching.

Lean and powerful, these dogs
are built for speed. Their long,
muscular legs can propel them at
up to 45 mph (70 km/h). At full
stretch, their streamlined movement is a joy to watch. The close,
fine coat comes in black, gray,
white, red, blue, fawn, fallow,
brindle or any color broken with
white. Those dogs now bred for
racing are slightly smaller than
those bred for pets.

■ TEMPERAMENT

Gentle and sensitive, the
Greyhound makes a surprisingly
docile and obedient pet, given its
hunting background. It does,

Fawn and white female
Greyhound. This breed is one
of the few that does not suffer
from genetic hip dysplasia.

owever, retain a well-developed hase instinct and should be muzzled and kept on a leash in public. Greyhounds are good with children and settle happily into the family routine. While these dogs are easily trained, owners must be careful not to break their spirit by being harsh or overbearing. They make good watchdogs.

■ GROOMING

Comb and brush the smooth, shorthaired coat with a firm bristle brush, and shampoo only when necessary. A rub with a chamois will make the coat gleam.

■ EXERCISE AND FEEDING

Pet Greyhounds must have long, brisk walks at the same time each day and opportunities to run free on fenced open ground. No special feeding needs, but it is best to feed two small meals a day rather than a single large one.

Irish Wolfhound

Size: male 28–38 in (71–95 cm)
female 26–34 in (66–86 cm)

Weight: male 90–120 lb (41–54 kg)
female 80–110 lb (36–50 kg)

■ ABOUT THIS BREED
A true gentle giant, the
Irish Wolfhound is
affectionate and makes a
wonderful family pet, although
it can be rather difficult and
expensive to look after. It was
once used to hunt wolves—so
successfully that wolves have
disappeared from the British Isles.

After working its way out of a
job, the breed was brought back
from the brink of extinction about
140 years ago by Captain George
Graham, a British Army officer,
who saw that it had great
potential for rescue work.

A massive, muscular-looking
dog, the Irish Wolfhound is the
tallest breed in the world. Its
rough, wiry coat comes in gray,
brindle, red, black, fawn and
white. The large, round paws
have markedly arched toes and
strong, curved toenails.

■ TEMPERAMENT
Despite being a killer of wolves,
this dog is gentle, loyal and very
affectionate. It is trustworthy

round children, although it
might knock them over with its
strong tail. While disinclined to
bark and sometimes shy, it makes
an adequate watchdog, because
its size alone makes it somewhat
daunting to intruders.

fawn male Irish Wolfhound

■ GROOMING
Unless the hard, wiry coat is
combed often, it will become
matted. Carefully clip out
any knots and trim around
the eyes and ears with blunt-
nosed scissors.

■ EXERCISE AND FEEDING
Given the chance, Irish
Wolfhounds are inclined to be
lazy. They need a reasonable
amount of exercise, but no
more than smaller breeds.
To avoid damage to
immature joints and bones,
do not take young dogs for
very long walks. There are
no special feeding
requirements.

Working Dogs

THIS ANCIENT GROUP INCLUDES BREEDS that date back to times when dogs were used to guard settlements, carry loads and engage in battle. There have been depictions of large Mastiff-type dogs for many thousands of years. Working dogs are generally large, strong and obedient. Some of them, such as the Doberman Pinscher, still make exemplary guard dogs. Others, such as the Saint Bernard, are used in rescue work. While some dogs within this group can be aggressive, they are unflinchingly loyal to their owners.

Shiba Inu

Size: male 14–16 in (36–41 cm)
female 13–15 in (33–38 cm)

Weight: male 20–30 lb (9–14 kg)
female 18–28 lb (8–13 kg)

■ ABOUT THIS BREED

The name Shiba possibly comes from a Japanese word for brushwood, or it may derive from an old word meaning small (*inu* means dog). Because of its convenient size and vivacious, outgoing personality, the Shiba Inu is now the most commonly owned pet dog in its native Japan and it is gaining in popularity world-wide. The Shiba is the smallest of the Japanese Spitz-type dogs and was originally bred to flush birds and small game from brushwood areas.

The Shiba looks like a much smaller version of the Akita (see p. 242). It has a strong, agile, well-proportioned body and alert bearing. The double coat usually comes in red tones, sable or black and tan, with pale shadings on the legs, belly, chest, face and tail.

■ TEMPERAMENT

Lively, good natured and very independent, Shibas are smart but can be difficult to train because they choose which commands to obey. They make good watchdogs but, although extremely sociable, can be aggressive to strange dogs.

GROOMING

Brush the coarse, stiff, shorthaired coat with a firm bristle brush, and bathe only when absolutely necessary as this removes the natural waterproofing of the coat.

EXERCISE AND FEEDING

This is an active dog needing lots of exercise. There are no special feeding requirements.

The handsome Shiba needs firm and consistent training from a young age. It digs and climbs with ease and, as a puppy, may wreak havoc on your house.

SNAPSHOT

PERSONALITY **Energetic, friendly, loyal, independent**
GROOMING **Regular brushing**
EXERCISE **Regular, moderate**
ENVIRONMENT **Ideal for urban or apartment living, but needs plenty of exercise**
BE AWARE **Hardy breed, with few genetic weaknesses; doesn't like to be left alone outside**

Red male Shiba. The waterproof, all-weather coat protects this dog in both cold and hot conditions.

Chow Chow

Size: male 18–23 in (46–56 cm)
female 18–22 in (46–53 cm)

Weight: male 50–65 lb (23–29 kg)
female 45–60 lb (20–27 kg)

■ ABOUT THIS BREED

An appealing, unusual-looking dog, the Chow Chow is less exuberant than many of its fellows, but nevertheless affectionate and loyal. It has a growing band of devotees around the world.

Physically very similar to fossilized remains of ancient dogs, the Spitz-type Chow Chow probably originated in Siberia or Mongolia. Used as a temple guard, it later became the favored hunting dog of Chinese emperors. It was almost unknown in the West until about 120 years ago.

The two most distinctive features of the Chow Chow are its blue-black tongue and its almost straight hind legs, which make its walk rather stilted. Its dense, furry, double coat is profuse and comes in solid black, red, fawn, cream, blue or white, sometimes with lighter or darker shades, but never particolored. The ears are small and rounded and there is a huge ruff behind the head, which gives it a lion-like appearance.

Black male Chow Chow

PERSONALITY **Independent, reserved; a one-person dog**
GROOMING **Regular brushing**
EXERCISE **Regular, moderate**
ENVIRONMENT **Adapts well to urban living, but needs space**
BE AWARE **Problems with hip and elbow dysplasia and prone to genetic eye diseases. Unsuited to life in hot climates**

■ TEMPERAMENT

Although a bit of a challenge to train, the strong-willed Chow Chow makes a good watchdog. It has a reputation for ferocity, probably undeserved, but is a tenacious fighter if provoked.

■ GROOMING

Regular brushing of the long outer coat is important to maintain the lifted, standing-out look. Extra care is needed when the dog is molting its dense undercoat. Dry shampoo when necessary.

■ EXERCISE AND FEEDING

Chow Chows can be lazy, but they will keep fitter if given regular moderate exercise. Don't overfeed.

Boxer

Size: male 22–24 in (56–61 cm)
female 21–23 in (53–58 cm)

Weight: male 60–70 lb (27–32 kg)
female 55–65 lb (25–29 kg)

■ ABOUT THIS BREED

If your best friend is a Boxer, you can rely on it absolutely to take good care of your property and to be waiting with the most enthusiastic welcome whenever you return home.

Developed in Germany from Mastiff-type dogs, the Boxer was originally used in bull-baiting and eventually crossed with the Bulldog to improve its ability in this field. It was little known outside its country of origin until after World War II, when British and American soldiers returned home with some of these brave and handsome animals.

The body is compact, muscular and powerful. The shiny, close-fitting coat comes in fawn, brindle and various shades of red, marked with white. The tail is usually docked short, so the whole hindquarters wag in greeting.

■ TEMPERAMENT

Intelligent and easily trained, Boxers have been widely used in military and police work. Training should start young and be firm and consistent—these exuberant animals need to be handled by a strong adult. They are reliable and protective with children and intensely loyal to their family. Excellent watchdogs, they will restrain an intruder in the same way a Bulldog does.

■ GROOMING

Brush the smooth, shorthaired coat with a firm bristle brush, and bathe only when necessary. Check out skin lumps discovered during grooming in case they are tumors.

■ EXERCISE AND FEEDING

An active, athletic breed, Boxers need daily work or exercise. As well as a long, brisk, daily walk, they enjoy a session of play, such as fetching a ball. There are no special feeding requirements.

SNAPSHOT

PERSONALITY **Lively, loving, loyal**
GROOMING **Daily brushing**
EXERCISE **Regular, vigorous**
ENVIRONMENT **Adapts well to urban living, but needs space**
BE AWARE **Prone to skin cancer, so check out any skin lumps; also genetic heart problems. The shape of the nose can lead to sinus infections and breathing difficulties**

Brindle and white male Boxer. This breed may be aggressive with other dogs.

Schnauzer

Standard
Size: male 18–20 in (46–51 cm)
female 17–19 in (43–48 cm)

Weight: male 40–45 lb (18–20 kg)
female 35–40 lb (16–18 kg)

Giant
Size: male 26–28 in (66–71 cm)
female 23–26 in (58–66 cm)

Weight: male 60–80 lb (27–36 kg)
female 55–75 lb (25–34 kg)

■ ABOUT THIS BREED
The Schnauzer (once known as the Wirehaired Pinscher) is an ancient German breed, or more correctly, three breeds, since the three sizes are considered separate breeds. In the United States, the Giant and Standard are classified as working dogs while the Miniature (see p. 158) is included with terriers. Many countries class all three together in the utility dog group. The Giant was originally used for herding cattle and as a guard dog. It was later harnessed to pull small traps. The Standard was prized as a ratter and often accompanied the stage coaches. An angular, square-looking dog, strong and vigorous, the Schnauzer has a hard, wiry, double coat that comes in pure black or salt and pepper colors, sometimes with white on the chest. The thick eyebrows and long mustache are often trimmed to accentuate the dog's overall square-cut shape. The feet are neat, round and compact, with well-arched toes and thick black pads. The tail is usually docked at the third joint.

■ TEMPERAMENT
These dogs are noted for their reliability and affectionate nature and they make excellent

Salt and pepper male
Standard Schnauzer

SNAPSHOT

PERSONALITY **Intelligent, spirited, lively, affectionate**
GROOMING **Daily brushing**
EXERCISE **Regular, moderate**
ENVIRONMENT **Adapts well to urban living; needs space to run**
BE AWARE **Subject to genetic eye diseases; also hip dysplasia and orthopedic problems**

watchdogs. They need firm, consistent training because they are inclined to be headstrong.

■ GROOMING

See general directions for wiry coats p. 42. These dogs should be professionally clipped to an even length twice a year.

■ EXERCISE AND FEEDING

Schnauzers relish play sessions and a run off the leash. Don't overdo it with a young pup, until the frame is strong and mature. There are no special feeding requirements.

Black male Giant Schnauzer.
The name comes from *Schnauze*, the German word for muzzle, a reference to the distinctive mustache of this breed.

Samoyed

Size: male 20–22 in (51–56 cm)
female 18–20 in (46–51 cm)

Weight: male 45–55 lb (20–25 kg)
female 40–50 lb (18–23 kg)

■ ABOUT THIS BREED
The Samoyed is almost
always good-humored and
up to any challenge. With its
pale, luxurious fur coat and
thick, perky tail curled over the
back to one side, it makes a
spectacular pet. (It is difficult,
however, to find ticks in the
dense, woolly undercoat.)

Samoyeds are members of
the Spitz family of dogs, whose
members are found throughout
Arctic regions. They evolved as
pack animals and sled dogs and
were used by the nomadic
Samoyed tribe of Siberia.

The compact muscular body of
this hard-working breed indicates
its strength. The thick, silver-
tipped coat, which comes in
white, biscuit and cream, makes
them unsuited to hot climates.
They are given to digging holes
in which they lie to cool off.

■ TEMPERAMENT
The Samoyed is too friendly to
be of much use as a watchdog,
but its bark will at least alert you
to the presence of strangers.

Start training at an early age. It gets on well with children and adapts well to family life.

■ GROOMING
Brushing two or three times a week is usually all that is needed, but extra care will be necessary when the dog is molting. The long coat does not shed, but the woolly undercoat comes out in clumps twice a year. Bathing is difficult and mostly unnecessary, as the coat sheds dirt readily. Dry shampoo from time to time by brushing unscented talcum powder through the coat.

■ EXERCISE AND FEEDING
Samoyeds need a reasonable amount of exercise, but take it easy during warm weather because the woolly undercoat inhibits loss of the heat built up during exercise. There are no special feeding requirements, but Samoyeds are particularly fond of fish.

White female Samoyed

SNAPSHOT

PERSONALITY Gentle, friendly, good-natured
GROOMING Brush twice weekly; more when molting
EXERCISE Regular, moderate
ENVIRONMENT Adapts to urban living, but needs space to run
BE AWARE Particularly prone to hip dysplasia; also suffers from diabetes. Unsuited to very hot climates

Sled Dogs

Siberian Husky
Size: male 21–23 in (53–58 cm)
      female 20–22 in (51–56 cm)

Weight: male 45–60 lb (20–27 kg)
        female 35–50 lb (16–23 kg)

Alaskan Malamute
Size: male 25–28 in (63–71 cm)
      female 23–26 in (58–66 cm)

Weight: male 90–115 lb (41–52 kg)
        female 85–110 lb (38–50 kg)

■ ABOUT THESE BREEDS
Both of these breeds are strong, compact working dogs. Siberian Huskies usually have a white face mask and underbody, with the remaining coat any color. Mismatched eyes are common. The large "snow-shoe" feet have hair between the toes for grip on ice. In Malamutes, the underbody and face masking is always white, while the remaining coat may be light gray to black, gold to red and liver. The plumed tail is carried over the back.

■ TEMPERAMENT
Because both breeds are friendly with people and bark little, they are ineffective as

Gray and white male Siberian Husky. Lack of exercise will make these dogs restless; if not securely enclosed, they will go off hunting by themselves.

watchdogs, although their size and intimidating appearance may deter intruders. Malamutes may be aggressive with other dogs.

GROOMING

Brush these dense, coarse coats twice a week, with extra care during molting—the undercoat comes out in clumps twice a year. Bathing is mostly unnecessary, as the coat sheds dirt readily. Dry shampoo occasionally.

EXERCISE AND FEEDING

Siberian Huskies need a fair amount of exercise, but don't overdo it in warm weather. They need a large yard with a high fence, but bury wire at the base of the fence because they are likely to dig their way out and go off hunting. Huskies are thrifty feeders and need less food than you might expect. However, they tend to wolf down whatever is offered, which can lead to obesity and bloat.

Wolf gray male Alaskan Malamute. These sledding dogs of the Spitz family were named after a nomadic Inuit tribe from Alaska, the Malhemut.

Rottweiler

Size: male 25–27 in (63–69 cm)
female 23–25 in (58–63 cm)

Weight: male 100–135 lb (45–61 kg)
female 90–120 lb (41–54 kg)

■ ABOUT THIS BREED

Strong and substantial, the
Rottweiler is not a dog for
inexperienced owners nor for
the average home. It makes an
imposing and effective guard
dog but needs firm handling and
proper training. The forebears
of this breed were left behind
throughout Europe many
centuries ago when the Roman
army withdrew. In the area
around Rottweil, in southern
Germany, these mastiff-type
animals were crossed with
sheepdogs to produce "butchers'
dogs" capable of herding and
guarding livestock.

Compact, muscular dogs,
Rottweilers have surprising speed
and agility. The thick, medium-
length coat is always black with
rich tan to mahogany markings. It
conceals a fine undercoat. The tail
is usually docked at the first joint.

■ TEMPERAMENT

Rottweilers are prized for their
aggression and guarding abilities,
yet, with proper handling, they
can also be loyal, loving and very

rewarding companions. They are highly intelligent and have proved their worth beyond doubt in police, military and customs work over the centuries. Training must begin while the dog is still small, and great care should be taken to ensure that it is not made either fearful or vicious.

■ GROOMING
Brush the smooth, glossy coat with a firm bristle brush, and bathe only when necessary.

■ EXERCISE AND FEEDING
You can't give these robust dogs too much work or exercise—they thrive on it. No special feeding requirements, but avoid over-feeding and do not exercise after a meal.

Black and tan male Rottweiler. Dogs of this breed are formidable animals. They need kind and consistent training from a strong adult if they are to be kept under control and should always be muzzled and kept on a leash in public places.

Akita

Size: male 21–24 in (53–61 cm)
female 19–22 in (48–56 cm)

Weight: male 90–110 lb (41–50 kg)
female 85–105 lb (38–48 kg)

■ ABOUT THIS BREED
The national dog of Japan, many champions of this breed are considered national treasures. The handsome and much-loved Akita is renowned for its strength, courage and loyalty.

The Akita has only recently become known outside its native Japan, where it was used for hunting deer, wild boar and black bears. In feudal times, it was pitted in savage dog-fighting spectacles, but these are now outlawed and the dog has found work with the police and as a reliable guard dog.

Displaying characteristics that are typical of the Spitz family, to which it belongs, the Akita is the largest of the Japanese Spitz-type breeds. It has a well-proportioned muscular body and a waterproof double coat that comes in all colors with clear, dark markings.

The tail is thick and carried in a curl or double curl over the back. Akitas have webbed feet and are very strong swimmers.

TEMPERAMENT

Despite the ferocity of many of its past activities, the Akita can, with proper socialization as a puppy and diligent training, make a very good pet. They also make excellent watchdogs. Always take care, however, around other dogs.

Red and white male Akita

GROOMING

The coarse, stiff, shorthaired coat requires a significant amount of grooming and is shed twice a year. Brush with a firm bristle brush, and bathe only when absolutely necessary as bathing removes the natural waterproofing of the coat.

EXERCISE AND FEEDING

The Akita needs moderate but regular exercise to stay in shape. There are no special feeding requirements.

Bernese Mountain Dog

Size: male 24–28 in (61–71 cm)
female 23–27 in (58–69 cm)

Weight: male 85–110 lb (38–50 kg)
female 80–105 lb (36–48 kg)

■ ABOUT THIS BREED

Once used as an all-round working dog in its native Switzerland, the Bernese Mountain Dog adapts easily to domestic life as long as it is given plenty of loving attention from the whole family.

Also known as the Bernese Sennenhund, these dogs made themselves useful herding cattle, guarding farms and pulling carts in a specially made harness. They also share the Saint Bernard's skill at finding people lost in the snow. This breed is one of four Swiss breeds that probably originated in Roman times.

A large, powerful dog, the handsome Bernese is vigorous and agile. It has a thick, gleaming, soft, wavy black coat with white and chestnut markings. It is best suited to a cool climate.

■ TEMPERAMENT

These gentle, cheerful dogs love children. They are very intelligent, easy to train and are naturally excellent watchdogs. They are very loyal and may have

trouble adjusting to a new owner after they are 18 months old.

■ GROOMING
Daily brushing of the long, thick, silky coat is important, with extra care needed when the dog is molting. Bathe or dry shampoo as necessary. Clip in summer in hot climates.

Tricolor male
Bernese
Mountain Dog

■ EXERCISE AND FEEDING
Large, active dogs such as these need a regular exercise regimen. There are no special feeding requirements.

SNAPSHOT

PERSONALITY **Placid, cheerful, loving, intelligent**
GROOMING **Daily brushing**
EXERCISE **Regular, moderate**
ENVIRONMENT **Adapts well to urban living, but needs plenty of regular exercise**
BE AWARE **Prone to hip and elbow dysplasia; also hereditary eye diseases and cancer**

Saint Bernard

Size: male 27 in (69 cm) or more
female 25 in (63 cm) or more

Weight: male from 172 lb (80 kg)
female from 160 lb (72 kg)

■ ABOUT THIS BREED
Saint Bernards are named after Bernard de Menthon, the founder of a famous hospice built in a remote alpine pass in Switzerland nearly 1,000 years ago. These sure-footed dogs have probably been used for rescue work since the seventeenth century.

With these very large, strong dogs, the taller the dog is, the better, as long as the weight is in proportion to the height. There are two types of coat, rough and smooth; both are very dense and come in white with markings in tan, mahogany, red, brindle and black in various combinations. The face and ears are usually shaded with black and the expression is intelligent and gentle. In rough-coated animals, the hair is slightly longer and there is feathering on the thighs and legs. The rough coat is a modern development, but since it ices up in extreme weather, it makes the dogs less suited to their original environment. The feet are

Smooth coat red and white male Saint Bernard. Bear in mind that an unruly dog of this size presents a control problem even for a strong adult, so training should begin early.

large, with strong, well-arched toes. These dogs have a highly developed sense of smell and seem to have a sixth sense about impending danger from storms and avalanches.

■ TEMPERAMENT

Dignified and reliable, the Saint Bernard is generally good with children and makes a good watchdog. It is highly intelligent and easy to train.

■ GROOMING

Comb and brush both types of coat with a firm bristle brush, and bathe only when necessary with mild soap—shampoo may strip the coat of its natural oils and water-resistant properties.

■ EXERCISE AND FEEDING

Short walks and brief play sessions are best until the dog's bones are mature, at about two years of age.

As these dogs are prone to bloat, feed them two or three small meals a day instead of one large one.

SNAPSHOT

PERSONALITY **Placid, affectionate**
GROOMING **Daily brushing; clean the eyes and wipe away dribble**
EXERCISE **Regular, moderate**
ENVIRONMENT **Well-suited to urban living if given plenty of exercise; unsuited to hot climates**
BE AWARE **Subject to hip dysplasia, epilepsy, bloat, skin problems and out-turned eyelids (ectropion)**

Mastiffs

Mastiff
Size: male from 30 in (76 cm)
female from 27 in (69 cm)

Weight: male from 160 lb (72 kg)
female from 150 lb (68 kg)

Bullmastiff
Size: male 25–27 in (63–69 cm)
female 24–26 in (61–66 cm)

Weight: male 110–133 lb (50–60 kg)
female 90–110 lb (41–50 kg)

■ ABOUT THESE BREEDS
The large, powerful Mastiff is an imposing sight. The shorthaired coat is dense, coarse and flat-lying and comes in shades of apricot, silver, fawn or darker fawn brindle. The muzzle, ears and nose are black and the wide-set eyes are hazel to brown. The Bullmastiff is smaller and more compact. The dense, coarse, water-resistant coat comes in dark brindle, fawn and shades of red. The face and neck are darker and deeply folded. Sometimes there are white marks on the chest.

Fawn female Mastiff. In former times, these ferocious and formidable fighters were often used for military work as well as hunting, but these magnificent animals also have a gentle side.

TEMPERAMENT

An exceptional guard dog, the Mastiff must be handled firmly and trained with kindness if it is to be kept under control. Properly handled, it is docile, good natured and loyal, but it can become a big problem if it gets the upper hand. Although the Bullmastiff is unlikely to attack, it will catch an intruder, knock him down and hold him. At the same time, it is tolerant of children, even-tempered, calm and loyal. It rarely barks or loses its temper.

GROOMING

Brush the Mastiff's smooth, shorthaired coat with a firm bristle brush and wipe over with a piece of toweling or chamois for a gleaming finish. Comb and brush the Bullmastiff's shorthaired, slightly rough coat with a firm bristle brush. There is little shedding with this breed. Shampoo both breeds only when necessary. Check the feet regularly, because they carry a lot of weight, and trim the toenails.

Fawn male Bullmastiff

SNAPSHOT

PERSONALITY **Courageous, loyal, reliable**
GROOMING **Daily brushing**
EXERCISE **Regular, moderate**
ENVIRONMENT **Adapts to urban living, but needs space to exercise**
BE AWARE **Both breeds are susceptible to bloat, hip dysplasia and some eye problems. Don't like weather extremes**

■ EXERCISE AND FEEDING

These breeds are inclined to be lazy but will keep happier and fitter if given regular exercise. Always keep on a leash in public. As they are prone to bloat, feed two or three small meals a day, instead of one large one.

Doberman Pinscher

Size: male 25–27 in (63–69 cm)
female 23–26 in (58–66 cm)

Weight: male 55–75 lb (25–34 kg)
female 50–70 lb (23–32 kg)

■ ABOUT THIS BREED
Originally developed to deter
thieves, the Doberman Pinscher
is prized as an obedient and
powerful watchdog, but with
proper training from puppyhood,
it can also become a devoted
family pet.

These fearless and intimidating
dogs were developed late in the
nineteenth century by a German
tax collector, Louis Dobermann.
He drew on a number of breeds,
including Rottweilers, German
Pinschers, German Shepherds and
Manchester Terriers, to produce
the ultimate guard dog—obedient
and courageous.

The Doberman Pinscher is
an elegant, muscular and very
powerful dog. It has a well-
proportioned chest, a short back
and a lean, muscular neck. Its
hard, shorthaired, close-fitting
coat generally comes in black, or

black and tan, although blue-gray,
red and fawn also occur. Because
of its short coat, it should never
be exposed to extreme cold.

Black and tan female
Doberman Pinscher

TEMPERAMENT

This breed's reputation for aggression is generally undeserved, but firm and determined training from puppyhood is essential. Fortunately, these dogs are easy to school and they make loyal and obedient watchdogs. As well as being fearless, they are alert, agile and energetic. Because they are powerful animals, always watch when they are with small children.

SNAPSHOT

PERSONALITY **Intelligent, loyal and fearless, but may be aggressive**
GROOMING **Daily brushing**
EXERCISE **Regular, vigorous**
ENVIRONMENT **Adapts to urban living if given enough exercise**
BE AWARE **Subject to such common diseases as bloat, hip dysplasia and eye problems; also prone to heart disease**

GROOMING

The smooth, shorthaired coat is easy to groom. Comb and brush with a firm bristle brush, and shampoo only when necessary. Wipe over with a damp cloth or chamois to make the coat gleam.

EXERCISE AND FEEDING

These dogs are very active, requiring plenty of daily exercise. They are not suitable for apartments or houses with small yards. Because they are prone to bloat, feed these dogs two or three small meals a day rather than one large one. Do not exercise straight after a meal.

Great Pyrenees

Size: male 25–32 in (63–81 cm)
female 23–30 in (58–76 cm)

Weight: male 100–130 lb (45–59 kg)
female 90–120 lb (41–54 kg)

■ ABOUT THIS BREED

The Great Pyrenees is a truly majestic animal that always impresses, but consider the commitment you are making carefully—you must have the space, patience and, most important, time to meet all its needs. Also known as the Pyrenean Mountain Dog, the Great Pyrenees is thought to have been used as a dog of war in ancient times when its temperament was less gentle than it is now. It also has a long history in its native France as a guard dog of sheep and châteaux.

Fully grown, this is a very large animal with a solid, muscular body. The long, coarse outer coat is either straight or slightly wavy; the fine undercoat is soft and thick. The waterproof coat is solid white or white with patches of tan, wolf-gray or pale yellow.

■ TEMPERAMENT

Although it is gentle and has a natural instinct for guarding, you should start a serious training

program for a young Great
Pyrenees when it is quite small.
These dogs make good watchdogs.

■ GROOMING
Regular brushing of the long
double coat will keep it in good
condition, but extra care is
needed when the dog is molting

SNAPSHOT

PERSONALITY Gentle, obedient,
loyal, affectionate
GROOMING Regular brushing
EXERCISE Regular, extensive
ENVIRONMENT Adapts well to
urban living, but needs plenty of
space and exercise
BE AWARE Problems with
orthopedic diseases, hip
dysplasia, genetic eye
diseases and deafness

its dense undercoat. The
outer coat doesn't mat, so
care is relatively easy.
Bathe or dry shampoo
only when necessary.

■ EXERCISE AND
FEEDING
These dogs don't reach
maturity until about two
years of age. They need
plenty of regular, though
not necessarily vigorous,
exercise to stay in shape.
They have no special
feeding requirements,
but growing puppies
require plenty of calcium,
preferably in the form of
sterilized bonemeal.

White female Great
Pyrenees. These dogs will
feel more comfortable in hot
summer weather if they are
clipped.

Newfoundland

Size: male 27–29 in (69–74 cm)
female 25–27 in (63–69 cm)

Weight: male 138–150 lb (63–68 kg)
female 110–120 lb (50–54 kg)

■ ABOUT THIS BREED
The Newfoundland, one
of the few dogs native
to North America,
did invaluable work
for early settlers pulling
sleds, hunting and guard-
ing. A naturally powerful
swimmer, the Newfoundland
has an outstanding record of
sea rescues to its credit. It was
prized by fishermen in its region
of origin, along the east coast
of Canada.

This massive dog comes in
black, browns, or black with
white markings—this variant
being known as the Landseer
after its depiction in a painting
by Sir Edwin Landseer. Like
some other water-loving breeds,
the Newfoundland has webbing
between the toes. The thick coat
makes the breed quite unsuited
to life in a hot climate.

■ TEMPERAMENT
Famous as the "Nana" dog in
Peter Pan, these dogs are noted
for being gentle with children, but
pups must be taught not to be
clumsy before they grow too

Black male
Newfoundland

large. They are adaptable, loyal and courageous, with great strength and endurance, and make good watchdogs.

■ GROOMING
Daily brushing of the thick, coarse, double coat with a hard brush is important. The undercoat is shed once or twice a year and

SNAPSHOT

PERSONALITY Intelligent, gentle, loyal, courageous
GROOMING Daily brushing
EXERCISE Regular, moderate
ENVIRONMENT Adapts well to urban living, but needs plenty of space to run free
BE AWARE Hip dysplasia and other orthopedic problems are common, also genetic heart conditions

extra care is required at these times. Avoid bathing unless really necessary, as this strips the coat of its natural oils. Instead, dry shampoo occasionally.

■ EXERCISE AND FEEDING
This gentle giant is quite content to laze around the house, but will benefit from regular moderate exercise and frequent opportunities to swim and play. There are no special feeding needs, but don't overfeed.

Great Dane

Size: male 30–32 in (76–81 cm)
female 28–30 in (71–76 cm)

Weight: male 100–125 lb (45–57 kg)
female 90–105 lb (41–48 kg)

■ ABOUT THIS BREED
Ancestors of this aristocratic breed have been known in Germany, where they probably originated, for more than 2,000 years. Despite their size, they are surprisingly gentle. Among the tallest of all dog breeds, the powerful, fast and agile Great Dane was originally favored by the German aristocracy for hunting boar and stags.

These large, tall, muscular dogs come in fawn, striped brindle, black, blue and harlequin.

■ TEMPERAMENT
Gentle, loyal, affectionate, playful and patient with children, the Great Dane is well behaved and makes a very good watchdog—its size alone would be daunting to an intruder. Start on a training program before your Great Dane puppy grows too large.

■ GROOMING

The smooth, shorthaired coat is easy to groom. Comb and brush with a firm bristle brush, and dry shampoo when necessary. Bathing this giant is a major chore, so it pays to avoid the need by daily grooming. The toenails must be kept trimmed.

SNAPSHOT

PERSONALITY Gentle, loyal, playful, affectionate, sometimes shy
GROOMING Daily brushing
EXERCISE Regular, moderate
ENVIRONMENT Adapts well to urban living, but needs plenty of space to run free
BE AWARE Susceptible to bloat, hip dysplasia, bone cancer and some genetic heart problems

■ EXERCISE AND FEEDING

Great Danes need plenty of exercise, at the very least a long daily walk. Being very large and heavy dogs, they are prone to bloat, so feed small helpings two or three times a day rather than one large meal. Ideally, the dog's food dish should be raised so that the dog can eat without having to splay its legs. Avoid exercise after meals. Puppies should have plenty of calcium while they are growing, preferably in the form of sterilized bonemeal.

Fawn female Great Dane

Herding Dogs

WHILE NOT AS ANCIENT as some of the hounds, herding dogs have been used for thousands of years to protect livestock from predators and to keep them from straying. Herding dogs tend to be very nimble and intelligent and to have great stamina. Today, many of these dogs are still employed in their traditional roles, although they also make wonderful pets if given sufficient exercise and attention.

Shetland Sheepdog

Size: male 13–15 in (33–38 cm)
female 12–14 in (30–36 cm)

Weight: male 14–18 lb (6–8 kg)
female 12–16 lb (5–7 kg)

■ ABOUT THIS BREED

The Sheltie, as it is affectionately known, is well endowed with both beauty and brains. Intuitive and responsive to its owner's wishes, it makes a charming pet, becoming deeply attached to its family. This beautiful dog looks like a small version of the Collie (see p. 274), but it has developed over centuries on the Shetland Islands where it was used for herding sheep. Other Shetland animals, notably ponies and sheep, are also miniaturized.

Strong, nimble and lightly built, the Sheltie is a fast runner and can jump well. The most common colors for the long, shaggy coat are sable, blue merle and tricolor, but it also comes in black with white or tan. (The breed is generally healthy, but blue merles should be checked for any signs of deafness.)

■ TEMPERAMENT

Alert and remarkably intelligent, the sensitive Sheltie likes to feel that it is part of the family. It is easy to train, but may be shy with strangers. Excessive barking can be a problem with this breed, but it makes a good watchdog.

■ GROOMING

The coat is easier to care for than you might expect, but regular brushing is important. Mist the coat lightly with water before you begin and tease out mats before they get bad. Use the comb sparingly. The dense undercoat is shed twice a year, in spring and fall. The coat readily sheds dirt and mud and Shelties are quite fastidious about their cleanliness.

SNAPSHOT

PERSONALITY Obedient, loyal, intelligent, gentle
GROOMING Regular brushing
EXERCISE Regular, moderate
ENVIRONMENT Ideal for apartment living, but needs space to run
BE AWARE Generally healthy, but some cataracts and PRA, as well as liver and skin disease. Check blue merle pups for signs of deafness

Bathe or dry shampoo only when absolutely necessary. Take note that these dogs are sensitive to some heartworm preventatives.

■ EXERCISE AND FEEDING

This active, graceful dog needs lots of exercise, preferably running free. There are no special feeding requirements, but it's best to avoid obesity. Because the thick coat often disguises changes in body shape, check for weight increase by feeling the waist regularly.

Tricolor male Shetland Sheepdog

Corgis

Pembroke Welsh Corgi
Size: male 10–12 in (25–30 cm)
female 10–12 in (25–30 cm)

Weight: male 20–24 lb (9–11 kg)
female 18–22 lb (8–10 kg)

Cardigan Welsh Corgi
Size: male 10–13 in (25–33 cm)
female 10–13 in (25–33 cm)

Weight: male 20–26 lb (9–12 kg)
female 18–24 lb (8–11 kg)

■ ABOUT THESE BREEDS
Pembroke and Cardigan Welsh
Corgis have been considered
separate breeds for only about
70 years. The origins of both are
open to conjecture, but the
Pembroke is thought to have been
taken to Wales from Belgium by
weavers about 1,000 years ago.
Both breeds have long, powerful
little bodies set on short, well-
boned legs. The Pembroke's soft,
medium-length coat comes in red,
sable, fawn, tan and black, all
with or without white. The
Cardigan's wiry coat is of medium
length and comes in any color,
except pure white. Both are water-
resistant. The main difference is
in the tails. The Pembroke's is
quite short or docked very close
to the body. The
Cardigan has a
long, thick tail. It

Sable female
Pembroke
Welsh Corgi

also has a slightly longer body and larger, more widely spaced ears.

■ TEMPERAMENT

Because their way of getting sheep or cattle to move is to nip at their heels, Corgis have a tendency to nip people, too. This trait should be firmly discouraged from an early age. Both breeds are wary of strangers and make very good watchdogs.

■ GROOMING

Comb and brush either coat with a firm bristle brush, and bathe only when necessary. The coat is shed freely twice a year.

■ EXERCISE AND FEEDING

Naturally active little dogs, they should always be encouraged to remain so. No special feeding requirements; don't overfeed or they will become obese and lazy.

SNAPSHOT

PERSONALITY Affectionate, loyal, intelligent, independent
GROOMING Regular brushing
EXERCISE Regular, gentle
ENVIRONMENT Ideal for apartment living, if given plenty of exercise
BE AWARE Reasonably healthy, but short legs and a long back make Corgis prone to spinal disorders; also subject to genetic eye problems

Black and white male
Cardigan Welsh Corgi

Puli

Size: male 16–18 in (41–46 cm)
female 14–16 in (36–41cm)

Weight: male 25–35 lb (11–16 kg)
female 20–30 lb (9–14 kg)

■ ABOUT THIS BREED

The "dreadlocks" worn in such a carefree way by the Puli are a special adaptation to protect the animal from extremes of weather. In mature coat, these dogs are an amazing sight.

This fabulous dog is currently enjoying an unprecedented wave of popularity in its native Hungary, where it was originally prized as an excellent sheepdog and guard. Before this, it may have lived in Central Asia. Like a few other herding breeds, it jumps on or over the backs of the sheep while moving them along.

The wiry, medium-sized Puli is among the most unusual-looking dogs in the world. Its long, dense, water-resistant double coat falls in naturally matted cords, eventually reaching the ground and hiding the legs completely. The hair is usually black, often reddish or tinged with gray, but it also occurs in white, gray, or apricot. The gait is quick and skipping. The tail, of medium length and curled over the back, is sometimes docked.

■ TEMPERAMENT

Pulis, or more correctly Pulik, are agile, intelligent creatures that respond well to training—they are used successfully as police dogs in Hungary and make great companions and good watchdogs.

■ GROOMING

This coat does not shed and is often left in its natural state—simply separate the strands with your fingers from time to time.

The dog can be bathed when necessary, but disturb the cords as little as possible. Clean around the ears and eyes regularly. Some owners prefer to clip their dogs and not allow the coat to cord.

■ EXERCISE AND FEEDING

Pulik are energetic and lively and enjoy plenty of regular activity, but take it easy on hot days. There are no special feeding requirements, but don't overfeed.

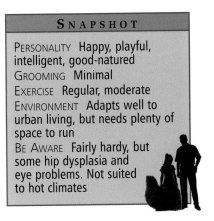

> ### SNAPSHOT
>
> PERSONALITY Happy, playful, intelligent, good-natured
> GROOMING Minimal
> EXERCISE Regular, moderate
> ENVIRONMENT Adapts well to urban living, but needs plenty of space to run
> BE AWARE Fairly hardy, but some hip dysplasia and eye problems. Not suited to hot climates

Black male Puli

Australian Cattle Dog

Size: male 17–20 in (43–51 cm)
female 17–19 in (43–48 cm)

Weight: male 32–35 lb (15–16 kg)
female 30–35 lb (14–16 kg)

■ ABOUT THIS BREED

The Australian Cattle Dog, also known as a Heeler, has in its make-up the best characteristics of its several antecedents. If you need a working dog, this is as good as they get.

A potent cocktail of blood runs in the veins of the Australian Cattle Dog: blue merle Collie, Dalmatian, Old English Sheepdog, Australian Kelpie, the little-known Smithfield and the native Dingo. The result is a working dog with few equals, ready, willing and able to drive cattle across vast distances under harsh, hot, dusty conditions. Both its guarding and herding instincts are very strong indeed and may extend to people and other pets.

This is not your average pampered pooch, but a tough, medium-sized dog that was bred for hard work. There are two coat colors: speckled blue, with tan or black markings, or speckled red, with dark red markings. Check

266 BREEDS

puppies and their relatives for signs of deafness before buying.

■ TEMPERAMENT
The Australian Cattle Dog is absolutely loyal and obedient to its master, but it is something of a one-person dog. It may also feel compelled to establish dominance over other dogs. It makes an excellent watchdog.

Blue, black and tan female Australian Cattle Dog

■ GROOMING
The coarse, shorthaired, weather-resistant coat needs little care and is very easy to groom. Just comb and brush with a firm bristle brush to distribute the natural oils through the coat, and bathe only when necessary.

■ EXERCISE AND FEEDING
These animals were bred to have incredible stamina under tough conditions and love to have a job to do. They will enjoy all the activity you can give them. Exercise is of paramount importance—without enough they can be bored and destructive. There are no special feeding requirements.

Border Collie

Size: male 18–21 in (46–53 cm)
female 17–20 in (43–51 cm)

Weight: male 30–45 lb (14–20 kg)
female 27–42 lb (12–19 kg)

■ ABOUT THIS BREED
Ready, willing and
able sums up the
Border Collie asleep
at your feet. You might
think that you have
succeeded in tiring
him out, but move a muscle
and he'll be instantly alert,
ready to learn a new trick.

Developed for herding sheep
in the rugged Scottish border
country, the Border Collie's speed
and stamina have made it an
outstanding worker and now
a favorite worldwide.

These athletic little dogs have
well-proportioned bodies, lean
and well-muscled. The medium-
length, double coat comes mainly
in black with white, sometimes
tricolored with tan, and also blue
merle with white markings. There
is often lavish feathering on the
legs, underbody and tail, and a

ruff behind the head. It is noted
for the way it can control sheep
with its eyes.

■ TEMPERAMENT
Highly intelligent and eager to
please, Border Collies are easily

obedience trained, but harsh training can make them submissive. They are wonderful pets, especially in homes with energetic children, but can be scrappy and jealous with other dogs. They make good watchdogs.

Black and white female Border Collie. These dogs must have enough exercise—boredom can lead to bad habits.

■ GROOMING
Regular combing and brushing will keep the coat gleaming, with extra care needed when the soft, dense undercoat is molting. Bathe or dry shampoo only when necessary. Check the ears and thick undercoat regularly for ticks.

■ EXERCISE AND FEEDING
Fast and agile, these lively little dogs have boundless energy and thrive on hard work and play. They are a delight to see streaking after a ball, or bringing straying sheep back to the fold. They also love to swim. No special feeding requirements, but don't allow them to become obese and lazy.

SNAPSHOT

PERSONALITY Intelligent, cooperative, joyful

GROOMING Regular brushing

EXERCISE Regular, vigorous

ENVIRONMENT Adapts well to urban living, but needs plenty of space for exercise

BE AWARE Generally hardy, but subject to some joint problems and genetic eye diseases, such as PRA

Australian Shepherd

Size: male 19–23 in (48–58 cm)
female 18–22 in (46–56 cm)

Weight: male 40–70 lb (18–32 kg)
female 35–65 lb (16–29 kg)

■ ABOUT THIS BREED

Highly regarded in farming circles as an outstanding working dog long before its official recognition as a breed, the Australian Shepherd is not yet widely appreciated beyond its home sphere. Despite the misleading name, it is not Australian at all but was developed entirely in the United States to work as a herding dog on ranches. The name may be derived from one of the dog's several ancestors.

The breed's principal forebears were probably Spanish dogs that accompanied Basque shepherds and herds of fine Merino sheep exported to both America and Australia in early colonial days. At some point, it was probably crossed with Collie stock.

A medium-sized dog, the Aussie, as it is known, has a lean, muscular body and a coarse, medium-to-long coat, which is well feathered on the ears, chest

and underbody, and the tops of the legs. There is a thick ruff on the chest and neck. The coat color and pattern are remarkably varied. The tail is very short or missing. If present, it is usually docked.

■ TEMPERAMENT
Extremely intelligent, easily trained and very responsive, these dogs seem to know exactly what

is required of them. They are very good watchdogs.

■ GROOMING
Brush the coat occasionally with a firm bristle brush, and bathe only when necessary.

■ EXERCISE AND FEEDING
This energetic working dog needs plenty of vigorous exercise to stay in shape, or better yet some real work to do. There are no special feeding requirements.

Black tricolor male Australian Shepherd

Bearded Collie

Size: male 21–22 in (53–56 cm)
      female 20–21 in (51–53 cm)

Weight: male 45–55 lb (20–25 kg)
       female 40–50 lb (18–23 kg)

■ ABOUT THIS BREED
A working sheepdog for most of its known history, especially in Scotland, these dogs were formerly called Highland Collies. They are thought to have developed from Polish Lowland Sheepdogs taken to Scotland about 500 years ago.

Well-proportioned and compact, the Bearded Collie looks a bit like a small Old English Sheepdog with an undocked tail. It has a shorter muzzle than other collies. The harsh, long double coat comes in all shades of gray, slate, black, red, brown and fawn, with or without white markings. There is a long, silky beard and abundant feathering.

■ TEMPERAMENT
Intelligent, responsive and alert, Bearded Collies are willing workers with great stamina and

endurance. They love children, but because of their size and herding instinct they may frighten

Slate male Bearded Collie. Consider carefully before buying a dog of this breed. While very attractive, they are fairly long-lived and take a lot of time and money to look after.

small children. They make good watchdogs but, if not well-trained when young, tend to bark a lot.

◼ GROOMING

Daily brushing of the long, shaggy coat is important—mist the coat lightly with water before you begin. Tease out mats before they get bad and give extra attention

when the dog is molting. Use the comb sparingly. If you prefer, the coat can be professionally machine clipped every two months or so. Bathe or dry shampoo when necessary. It is hard to locate ticks in the thick undercoat, so check regularly.

◼ EXERCISE AND FEEDING

This is an active dog that needs lots of exercise, preferably running free. No special feeding requirements.

Collie

Size: male 21–24 in (53–61 cm)
female 20–23 in (51–58 cm)

Weight: male 45–65 lb (20–29 kg)
female 40–60 lb (18–27 kg)

■ ABOUT THIS BREED
Instantly recognizable to
generations of children
who were brought up
watching the television
series *Lassie*, the Collie is
now one of the most popular
dogs in the world.

The Collie was used in the
Scottish Lowlands as a hard-
working sheepdog. Its name
derives from the term used for the
local black sheep, colleys. There
are two types, identical except
for the length of their coats: the
Rough Collie and the less
common Smooth Collie. The
Rough Collie is by far the more
popular variety and is generally
referred to simply as the Collie.
Its magnificent coat provides
protection from the cold.

A large, strong dog, the Collie
often has the typical markings of
white collar, chest, feet and tail

tip. The main colors of the long,
thick double coat are sable,
tricolor and blue merle. The head
is long and tapered, and the facial
expression is gentle and knowing.

TEMPERAMENT

Very sociable and dependent on human company, Collies can be aloof with strangers. They are family oriented and good with children. Intelligent and easy to train, they make good watchdogs but can be terrible barkers. They may be sensitive to some heartworm preventatives.

GROOMING

The spectacular stiff coat sheds dirt readily and a thorough weekly brushing will keep it in good condition. Take extra care when the soft, dense undercoat is being molted. Clip out any mats and bathe or dry shampoo as necessary.

EXERCISE AND FEEDING

The weatherproof Collie needs plenty of outdoor exercise, preferably some of it off the leash. There are no special feeding requirements, but do not overfeed.

Sable and white female Collie

Belgian Shepherd Dogs

Size: male 24–26 in (61–66 cm)
female 22–24 in (56–61 cm)

Weight: male 65–75 lb (29–34 kg)
female 60–70 lb (27–32 kg)

■ ABOUT THESE BREEDS
Similar to German Shepherds, with well-shaped heads and long muzzles, each variety of Belgian Shepherd is distinguished by its coat. The Groenendael has an abundant, glossy, longhaired, black coat, sometimes with small white markings. The Tervuren also has long hair, but comes in fawn, gray and mahogany and any shade in between. The hair is tipped with black and the mask and the tips of the ears are also black. Both of these dogs have a generous ruff around the neck, larger in the male. The Malinois is fawn to mahogany with the same black tips and shaded areas as the Tervuren, but the hair is shorter. It thickens to a deep collar around the neck. The Laekenois has similar coloring to the Malinois, but its short hair is harsh and wiry.

■ TEMPERAMENT
Essentially working dogs, Belgian Shepherds are reliable, obedient

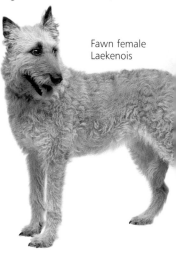

Fawn female
Laekenois

Fawn male
Tervuren

PERSONALITY Obedient, intelligent
GROOMING Regular brushing for shorthaired coats, more extensive for longhaired coats
EXERCISE Regular, vigorous
ENVIRONMENT Adapts to urban living, but needs space to run
BE AWARE Hardy and healthy, but some hip dysplasia and eye problems

and easily trained. Their training should always be patient, firm and consistent—if you are harsh or overbearing, they will become uncooperative. They are excellent police dogs and loyal pets.

■ GROOMING

Bathing is not recommended for these breeds, but dry shampoo if necessary. Otherwise, follow the general directions for grooming (see p. 42). The rough, wiry coat of the Laekenois needs only an occasional brushing with a firm bristle brush. It should be rough-looking but never curled.

■ EXERCISE AND FEEDING

These working dogs are used to an active outdoor life and like lots of exercise, preferably off the leash. No special feeding needs, but do not allow to become obese and lazy.

Black male
Groenendael

Fawn female
Malinois

Old English Sheepdog

Size: male 22–24 in (56–61 cm)
female 20–22 in (20–56 cm)

Weight: male from 65 lb (29 kg)
female from 60 lb (27 kg)

■ ABOUT THIS BREED

If you have endless patience and lots of time to spend grooming and exercising the Old English Sheepdog, your reward will be the love of a faithful and supremely glamorous companion.

Commonly called Bobtails, these dogs were developed for herding livestock, both sheep and cattle, in England's West Country. They are large, hardy, thickset, muscular dogs, with a distinctive low-pitched, loud, ringing bark. The shaggy coat is free of curls and comes in gray, grizzle, blue or blue merle, with or without white markings.

■ TEMPERAMENT

Playful and intelligent, Old English Sheepdogs learn quickly, but firm and consistent training should be started while the animal is still young and of a manageable size. They make good watchdogs, but if bored and lonely, they can be mischievous.

Gray and white male Old English Sheepdog

■ GROOMING

The coarse, longhaired coat needs constant care to keep it in top condition. It doesn't take long for it to get out of control. Unless it is combed and brushed through to the dense, waterproof undercoat at least three times a week, it will become matted and the dog may develop skin problems or be plagued by parasites. Clip out any tangles carefully so as not to nick the skin. A grooming table will make the whole job easier.

If you prefer, the coat can be professionally machine-clipped every two months or so. (In former times, these dogs were shorn along with the sheep.) Trim around the eyes and rear end with blunt-nosed scissors.

■ EXERCISE AND FEEDING

These dogs were developed for hard work and love a good run. There are no special feeding requirements.

SNAPSHOT

PERSONALITY Intelligent, playful, loyal, determined
GROOMING Daily, extensive
EXERCISE Regular, vigorous
ENVIRONMENT Adapts well to urban living, but needs plenty of space to run
BE AWARE Subject to hip dysplasia; also susceptible to genetic eye diseases. Not suited to hot climates

German Shepherd

Size: male 24–26 in (61–66 cm)
female 22–24 in (56–61 cm)

Weight: male 75–95 lb (34–43 kg)
female 70–90 lb (32–41 kg)

■ ABOUT THIS BREED

It seems as if the incredibly versatile German Shepherd can be trained to do any job. Admired the world over for its intelligence and excellence as a guard dog, it seems to thrive on a life of service.

Known also as Alsatians, German Shepherds were originally bred as herding dogs. Nowadays, their tasks include police, rescue, tracking and military work. They also make devoted companions.

Handsome, well proportioned and very strong, they must have firm and consistent handling by a strong adult and be trained to obedience from an early age. The coat most often comes in black with tan or fawn markings, but other colors do occur. The nose is always black.

■ TEMPERAMENT

These dogs seem ever-vigilant, are constantly on duty and make excellent watchdogs. They are both loved and feared, with good reason. They are inclined to be reserved until you win their

Black and tan female
German Shepherd

friendship, but from that time their loyalty is unquestioned. Time spent socializing puppies of this breed is of particular benefit (see p. 86) as they tend to be shy (fear can make them aggressive).

■ GROOMING

It is important to brush and comb the thick, coarse coat each day, and take extra care when the dog is molting its dense undercoat. At this time, the dead woolly hair clings to the new hair and must be removed with a slicker brush designed for the task. Bathe or dry shampoo only when necessary.

■ EXERCISE AND FEEDING

German Shepherds revel in strenuous activity, preferably combined with training of some kind or, best of all, a real job. As they are prone to bloat, it's best to feed two or three small portions instead of one large meal.

Briard

Size: male 23–27 in (58–69 cm)
female 21–25 in (53–63 cm)

Weight: male 70–80 lb (32–36 kg)
female 65–75 lb (29–34 kg)

■ ABOUT THIS BREED

A gentle giant, the Briard is now becoming better known and appreciated outside its native France, where it has for a long time been highly valued as an excellent working dog and devoted pet.

The breed's lineage goes back more than 1,000 years, although today's dog is more elegant than those of earlier times. It has long been regarded as a shepherd dog and, during World War I, allied soldiers fighting in France were impressed by its ability to carry messages and by the way it could pull supply wagons and locate those wounded in battle. It first appeared in the United States late in the eighteenth century.

A large, muscular animal, the Briard's gait is smooth and appears almost effortless. The long, shaggy coat comes in solid colors, especially black and fawns, the darker the better. The hind legs have double dewclaws.

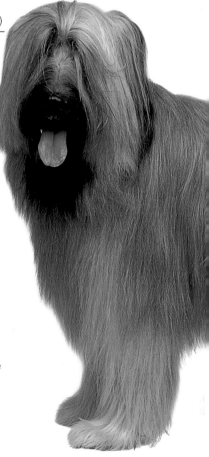

■ TEMPERAMENT

A long history of working with humans has made Briards sweet natured and gentle. They are intelligent and easy to train, making wonderful family pets and very good watchdogs. The herding instinct is strong.

■ GROOMING

If the dog is kept outside, the coat, which is non-shedding, seems largely to take care of itself. If the dog spends a lot of time indoors, you may wish to brush the long coat regularly and bathe or dry shampoo as necessary to reduce the "doggy" smell.

■ EXERCISE AND FEEDING

Briards are working dogs and must have plenty of vigorous exercise to keep them in top condition. No special feeding requirements, but don't let them become obese.

Fawn male Briard

Bouvier des Flandres

Size: male 23–28 in (58–71 cm)
female 22–27 in (56–69 cm)

Weight: male 75–90 lb (34–41 kg)
female 60–80 lb (27–36 kg)

■ ABOUT THIS BREED
Everything about the Bouvier des Flandres, or Ox-Drover of Flanders, says dependability— from its workmanlike body to its calm, steady manner. Today, its work includes police duties and guiding services for the blind.

The breed originated in pastoral regions around the Franco-Belgian border, where it was used for herding and guarding. During World War I, it was used as a messenger and to pull carts transporting wounded soldiers to hospital facilities.

Primarily a working dog, the Bouvier is powerful and short in the body. The rough, long, shaggy double coat comes in black, gray, brindle, salt and pepper, and fawn, sometimes with a white mark on the chest. A thick beard and mustache adorn the face. The tail is usually docked very short.

■ TEMPERAMENT
Steady, adaptable and even tempered, the Bouvier goes about

its business quietly and calmly. It is easy to train but can be very suspicious of strangers. It makes an excellent watchdog.

■ GROOMING

If the dog is kept outdoors, the harsh, dry coat seems to look after

itself, shedding dirt and water easily. If the animal lives in the house, you may wish to brush the long coat regularly and bathe or dry shampoo when necessary. This will certainly enhance the dog's appearance and both dog and owner will enjoy the contact. The coat can be trimmmed from time to time, if necessary.

Brindle male Bouvier des Flandres

■ EXERCISE AND FEEDING

Energetic and active, the Bouvier needs plenty of regular exercise. There are no special feeding requirements.

Non-Sporting Dogs

THIS GROUP CONTAINS BREEDS that don't fit neatly into any of the other categories. Some belong in this group because the task for which they were developed no longer exists. The Bulldog, for example, was bred for bull-baiting and then fighting, pastimes that are now outlawed. While dogs in this group have little in common, they are some of the most beautiful, intelligent and popular dogs today.

Bichon Frise

Size: male 9–11 in (23–28 cm)
female 9–11 in (23–28 cm)

Weight: male 11–16 lb (5–7 kg)
female 11–16 lb (5–7 kg)

■ ABOUT THIS BREED
It's easy to see why people are enchanted by the fluffy Bichon Frise. It loves to be the center of attention and is always eager to please—altogether a delightful and amusing companion.

Although it first came to notice as the darling of French royalty during the sixteenth century (*bichon* is French for lapdog; *frisé* means curly), the Bichon Frise is thought to have originated in the Canary Islands and was once called the Teneriffe. Its French or Belgian forebears may have been taken there by sailors.

This sturdy, confident little dog has a lively, prancing gait and a puffy white coat, sometimes with cream or apricot markings. The eyes are round and dark and the large, round nose is black. The tail is usually raised and curved, but never curled.

■ TEMPERAMENT
A gregarious individual, the Bichon Frise is playful and merry and not aggressive to people or other dogs. It is intelligent and easy to train. In spite of its small size, it is an effective watchdog.

White male
Bichon Frise

■ GROOMING

Daily brushing of the long, soft coat with a stiff bristle brush is essential. If neglected, the coat quickly becomes a sorry, matted mess. The fine, silky hair falls naturally in curls and is usually cut with scissors to follow the contours of the body and brushed out to a soft cloud. Dry shampoo as necessary and bathe once a month. Trim around the eyes and ears with blunt-nosed scissors and clean the eyes meticulously to prevent staining. Runny eyes, caused by blocked tear ducts, can stain the white coat. Ask your vet or a professional groomer about products that will remove these unsightly stains.

■ EXERCISE AND FEEDING

These are active little dogs and play will take care of most of their exercise needs, but they do love a walk and especially a romp in the open. There are no special feeding requirements.

Lhasa Apso

Size: male 10–11 in (25–28 cm)
female 9–10 in (23–25 cm)

Weight: male 14–18 lb (6–8 kg)
female 12–16 lb (5–7 kg)

■ ABOUT THIS BREED

This bewitching creature seems to be composed entirely of hair, but the Lhasa Apso is neither a toy nor a lapdog. It is a rugged little animal that earns its keep as a companion and watchdog.

Rarely seen outside Tibet until fairly recently, the Lhasa Apso was bred in monasteries as a temple and palace sentinel. It takes part of its name from the Tibetan capital, Lhasa.

This shaggy little dog looks like a small version of the Old English Sheepdog. Gold, creams and honey tones are the most popular colors, but the coat also comes in dark grizzle, smoke, slate and particolors of black, white or brown.

■ TEMPERAMENT

Adaptable, affectionate and loyal, these hardy little dogs thrive on human companionship and don't like to be left alone.

Their hearing is acute and they will alert you to any unusual sounds and to the approach of strangers. They are playful, intelligent, easily trained dogs and make delightful companions.

Cream male
Lhasa Apso

Slate male Lhasa Apso. It takes a lot of grooming to keep the coats of these dogs in peak condition. Some owners opt for easier care with a short all-over clip.

■ GROOMING

The long topcoat parts along the spine and falls straight on either side. Daily combing and brushing is vital. The thick undercoat will become matted if neglected. Dry shampoo as necessary. Check the feet for matting and for foreign matter stuck there. Clean eyes and ears meticulously.

■ EXERCISE AND FEEDING

Lhasa Apsos love to walk and scramble about and will be fitter and happier if given regular opportunities to run free and play. No special feeding needs, but clean any dribbles of food off the beard after each meal to avoid staining and matting.

Schipperke

Size: male 10–13 in (25–33 cm)
female 9–12 in (23–30 cm)

Weight: male 12–16 lb (5–7 kg)
female 10–14 lb (5–6 kg)

■ ABOUT THIS BREED
While the agile, hardy and independent little Schipperke (pronounced skipper-key) is remarkably self-sufficient, it is sociable, adapts well to family life and makes a well-behaved, loyal and affectionate pet.

Because Schipperkes tend to be very suspicious of strangers, they were popular watchdogs on Belgian barges, also keeping rats and mice in check. The name possibly derives from the Flemish for "little boatman." Schipperkes are probably related to the Groenendael, a Belgian Shepherd Dog (see p. 276).

These small dogs have a harsh double coat, usually black, but gold and some other solid colors do occur. The hair is smooth on the fox-like head, elsewhere more erect, and the male has a standing ruff around the neck. Schipperkes

are often born without a tail. If a tail is present, it is closely docked within a few days of birth.

■ TEMPERAMENT
This plucky little dog makes an excellent watchdog—it backs down for nobody. It is alert and

Black male
Schipperke

very curious, and nothing escapes its attention. Undemanding and devoted to its owner, it looks on itself as part of the family.

■ GROOMING

The Schipperke is particularly clean and pretty much takes care of its own grooming, but to keep the medium-length double coat in top condition, comb and brush regularly with a firm bristle brush. Dry shampoo only when really necessary.

■ EXERCISE AND FEEDING

In general, Schipperkes are an active breed. While some will be content with sessions of free play in a yard or park, others will want at least a long daily walk. There are no special feeding needs.

Boston Terrier

Size: male 11–15 in (28–38 cm)
female 11–15 in (28–38 cm)

Weight: male 15–25 lb (7–11 kg)
female 15–25 lb (7–11 kg)

■ ABOUT THIS BREED

Besides being an excellent watchdog, the Boston Terrier has much to recommend it—ease of care, handy size and a delightful disposition. No wonder it is one of the most popular breeds in the United States. Its direct forebears are English and French Bulldogs and the White English Terrier. It was developed in America only about 150 years ago as a fighting dog, a pastime that has since been outlawed. Although it is still always ready to scrap with other dogs, its behavior toward people is not aggressive.

Boston Terriers have compact and well-muscled bodies. Their faces are unmistakeable, with short, wide muzzles, prominent eyes set far apart and short, erect ears. The tail is short and fine. These dogs come in brindle or black, both with white markings.

■ TEMPERAMENT

Playful and very affectionate, they like to feel part of the family. They are intelligent, easy to train and quite reliable with children.

Brindle and white female Boston Terrier

■ GROOMING

The smooth, shorthaired, fine, glossy coat is easy to groom. Comb and brush with a firm bristle brush, and bathe only when necessary. Wipe the face with a damp cloth every day

and clean the prominent eyes carefully, as they are prone to injury. Check both the ears and eyes for grass seeds. Ticks may also lurk in the ears. The toenails should be clipped regularly.

■ EXERCISE AND FEEDING

These short-faced dogs may have breathing difficulties when stressed by exertion and hot or cold weather. Regular walks or sessions of free play in a fenced yard will help all Boston Terriers to stay in shape. There are no special feeding requirements.

Bulldog

Size: male 14–16 in (36–41 cm)
female 12–14 in (30–36 cm)

Weight: male 55–70 lb (25–32 kg)
female 48–60 lb (22–27 kg)

■ ABOUT THIS BREED
These stalwarts have come to epitomize determination and the broad-chested stance certainly suggests immovability, if not downright stubbornness. Yet Bulldogs make loving and lovable pets.

In earlier times, Bulldogs were fighting dogs that would take on opponents such as bulls, bears, badgers or even other dogs in the ring. When such bloodsports became unpopular, breeders concentrated on developing the breed's non-ferocious traits.

The coat comes in reds, fawn, brindle or fallow, or white pied with any of these colors. The muzzle is sometimes dark. With its stocky legs set squarely at each corner of its compact, muscular body, the Bulldog's deliberate gait has become a waddle.

■ TEMPERAMENT
Absolutely reliable, and although its appearance can be somewhat intimidating, it is among the gentlest of dogs. Just the same, it makes a very good watchdog and will see off any intruder—few would risk a close encounter with a dog brave enough to bait a bull.

Brindle and white male Bulldog

■ GROOMING

The smooth, fine, shorthaired coat is easy to groom. Comb and brush with a firm bristle brush, and bathe only when necessary. Wipe the face with a damp cloth every day as Bulldogs tend to drool (and snore), making sure that you clean inside the wrinkles.

■ EXERCISE AND FEEDING

Bulldogs are prone to chronic respiratory problems and would just as soon not take any exercise. They are stressed by exertion and hot or cold weather, but will stay fitter if given some regular, not overly strenuous activity such as walking. No special feeding requirements, but be careful not to overfeed them as they easily become obese. They can also be somewhat possessive of their food, which should be discouraged.

Poodle

Standard
Size: male 15–24 in (38–61 cm)
female 15–22 in (38–56 cm)

Weight: male 45–70 lb (20–32 kg)
female 45–60 lb (20–27 kg)

Miniature
Size: male 11–15 in (28–38 cm)
female 11–15 in (28–38 cm)

Weight: male 15–17 lb (7–8 kg)
female 15–17 lb (7–8 kg)

■ ABOUT THIS BREED
Poodles come in three sizes (for the Toy, the smallest, see p. 134). They are active, sure-footed dogs with excellent balance, moving lightly and easily with a sprightly, trotting gait. Their dense, woolly coats of springy curls are either brushed out to a soft cloud and

Cream female Standard Poodle. These dogs must be clipped every six to eight weeks, but many pet owners opt for a plain lamb clip, the same length all over, because it is easier and more economical to maintain than more traditional clips, such as this lion clip.

clipped, or simply combed for a more natural look. The fine, harsh-textured hair keeps growing and is not shed, which is why the Poodle is often chosen as a pet for people with allergies. The coat comes in solid white, cream, brown, apricot, black, silver and blue. Puppies' tails are usually docked at birth.

■ TEMPERAMENT
Considered by many the most intelligent of breeds, the Poodle

seldom becomes aggressive and has a great sense of fun.

■ GROOMING
Check ears frequently for mites and pull out hairs if necessary. Teeth need regular scaling by a vet.

■ EXERCISE AND FEEDING
Poodles will be fitter and keep in better spirits if allowed to run and play off the leash. Feed two or three small meals a day instead of one large one, and avoid exercise after meals.

Black male Miniature Poodle

Tibetan Terrier

Size: male 14–16 in (36–41 cm)
female 13–15 in (33–38 cm)

Weight: male 18–30 lb (8–14 kg)
female 16–25 lb (7–11 kg)

■ ABOUT THIS BREED
While it is treasured in its native
Tibet as a symbol of good luck,
you will probably cherish your
appealing little Tibetan Terrier
more for its delightful ways and
joyous zest for life.

Still something of a rarity in
Western countries, the Tibetan
Terrier was little known outside
Tibet until about 70 years ago. It
is not a true terrier as it does not
dig prey out of burrows. In its
homeland it is something of an
all-purpose farm dog.

This compact little animal is
nimble and sure-footed—it will
stand on its hind legs and jump
quite high to see what is on a
table, especially if it smells food.
The shaggy coat is fine and long,
falling over the eyes and face.
It comes in white, gold, cream,
gray shades, silver, black, tricolor
and particolor. The tail is well

feathered and is carried proudly
curled over the back.

■ TEMPERAMENT
These gentle, engaging animals
are easy to train, alert and full of
bravado. They will certainly let
you know if strangers are around.

Black, silver and
white male
Tibetan Terrier

These joyful little dogs always seem to be smiling and ready for a game.

■ GROOMING

Comb the long, double coat at least every second day with a metal comb to keep it free of tangles. The dense, fine, woolly undercoat is shed twice a year and extra care is needed during molting. Bathe or dry shampoo as necessary. Trim around the eyes with blunt-nosed scissors. Check and clean the ears regularly.

■ EXERCISE AND FEEDING

Sessions of play and regular walks will keep this lively dog fit and happy. No special feeding requirements, but if allowed they can become finicky about their food. They are good jumpers, so make your yard escape-proof.

Keeshond

Size: male 17–19 in (43–48 cm)
female 16–18 in (41–46 cm)

Weight: male 55–65 lb (25–29 kg)
female 50–60 lb (23–27 kg)

■ ABOUT THIS BREED

The Keeshond (pronounced kays-hond) is a great favorite in its native Netherlands, in spite of not being considered a pure-bred. It is a long-lived dog and becomes deeply attached to its owners.

Originally used as watchdogs on barges in Holland, the Keeshond was sometimes called the "smiling Dutchman" for its perpetual good-natured grin. It is a member of the Spitz group of dogs and has the typical tightly curled tail.

Keeshonden are compact, muscular animals with a cream or pale gray undercoat and a luxurious outer coat that comes in shades of gray with black tips, and stands away from the body. The markings are quite definite and there are distinctive pale "spectacles" around the eyes.

■ TEMPERAMENT

Reliable, adaptable, easy to care for and loyal to its family, the Keeshond is a natural watchdog and easy to train for other tasks.

Silver-gray male
Keeshond

■ GROOMING

Grooming the luxuriant, long coat is not as onerous as you might expect, but daily brushing with a stiff bristle brush is important. First, brush with the grain, then lift the hair with a comb, against

the grain, and lay it back in place. Bathe or brush a dry shampoo through the coat only when really necessary. Extra attention is needed twice a year, in spring and fall, when the dense undercoat is shed.

■ EXERCISE AND FEEDING

These dogs will readily adapt to any exercise regimen, whether it be demanding or easy, but they will keep fitter and be happier if given regular physical activity. Never use a choke chain as it will spoil the spectacular ruff. There are no special feeding requirements, but beware of overfeeding as these dogs tend to put on weight quickly and become lazy.

Shar Pei

Size: male 18–20 in (46–51 cm)
female 18–20 in (46–51 cm)

Weight: male 40–55 lb (18–25 kg)
female 40–55 lb (18–25 kg)

■ ABOUT THIS BREED

This ancient breed, also known as the Chinese Shar Pei, is thought to have originated in China about 2,000 years ago. The loose, wrinkled skin gives these dogs an appealingly worried, forlorn look. The breed almost became extinct during this century, but there was a resurgence of interest in the 1960s and they have now become very popular pets.

Both heavily wrinkled dogs with large heads and smaller-headed dogs with tighter-looking skins occur in this breed. The stiff, short, bristly coat feels rough to the touch and comes in black, red, fawn, apricot and cream, often with lighter tones on the backs of the hindquarters and tail. The small ears fall forward and the tail is carried in a curl. Like the Chow Chow, these dogs have a blue-black tongue.

■ TEMPERAMENT

Once used as fighting dogs, the well-mannered Shar Pei has a surprisingly friendly, easy-going

nature and makes a delightful companion, although it may be aggressive toward other dogs.

It needs firm but gentle training and makes a good watchdog.

■ GROOMING

Regular brushing with a bristle brush is often enough to keep the unusual coat in good condition, but these dogs are subject to chronic skin problems, including allergies, infections and mites. Keep an eye out during grooming sessions. Dry shampoo or bathe when necessary. They may require corrective eye surgery.

■ EXERCISE AND FEEDING

Shar Peis need regular exercise, but keep them on a leash in public. There are no special feeding requirements.

Apricot male Shar Pei

Dalmatian

Size: male 22–25 in (56–63 cm)
female 21–24 in (53–61 cm)

Weight: male 50–65 lb (23–29 kg)
female 45–60 lb (20–27 kg)

■ ABOUT THIS BREED

Exuberant and fun-loving, the Dalmatian is an excellent choice for anyone with the time to exercise and train it. Although it always turns heads, it is no mere fashion accessory.

The handsome Dalmatian's origins are obscure, but in nineteenth-century Europe, and particularly Britain, its main work was to run beside horse-drawn carriages. This may have been to protect the travelers inside or perhaps merely for appearance. It also kept the stables clear of rats.

A picture of elegance, the Dalmatian is of medium size with the lean, clean lines of the Pointer, to which it may be related. It is well muscled and has a short, hard, dense coat of pure white with well-defined, black or liver-colored spots randomly splashed over it. The feet are round with well-arched toes and the toenails are either white or the same color as the spots.

■ TEMPERAMENT

Spirited and playful, these dogs adore children and can be trusted with them. Training takes patience and gentle but firm and consistent handling, as they are rather sensitive. They make good watchdogs and like to spend time with their owners.

■ GROOMING

The smooth, lustrous, short-haired coat is easy to groom. Comb and brush with a firm bristle brush, and bathe only when necessary.

■ EXERCISE AND FEEDING

A Dalmatian is not an ideal dog for apartment dwellers unless it can be taken out for a brisk walk or run several times a day. It needs plenty of vigorous exercise or it may become bored and destructive. There are no special feeding requirements.

Black-spotted female Dalmatian. Newborn pups of this breed have no spots; the marks develop during the first year of life.

SNAPSHOT

PERSONALITY Gentle, sensitive, energetic, playful

GROOMING Daily brushing

EXERCISE Regular, vigorous

ENVIRONMENT Adapts well to urban living, but needs plenty of space to exercise

BE AWARE Some problems with skin allergies and urinary bladder stones; also prone to deafness

GLOSSARY

beard long, thick hair growing from the underside of the muzzle.

belton term used to describe the distinctive coloration of English Setters (white hairs flecked with blue, lemon, orange or liver).

bird dog a dog that tracks birds by scent.

bitch a female dog.

black and tan a common combination of black coat with tan markings.

blaze white marking down the nose or between the eyes.

blue paler shade of black coat.

blue merle blue-gray streaked with black.

bobtail a dog that either has no tail or whose tail has been docked very short.

brindle gray or tawny coat streaked with a darker color.

broken color solid color interspersed with another color.

chestnut medium-brown color.

chocolate dark fawn to brown color.

cobby relatively short from withers to hips.

cropping the practice of removing part of the ear to make it appear more erect; illegal in some states in the United States and in some other countries.

cross breeding the breeding together of two purebred dogs to create a mixed breed.

dewclaws a digit on the inside of dog's leg; if present at birth, those on back legs are usually removed.

dewlap loose, fleshy skin hanging below the throat.

docking the practice of removing part of the tail soon after birth; traditional for many breeds but discouraged in some countries.

double coat strong, resistant coat covering soft undercoat.

drop ear long, floppy ears that hang down.

ectropion damage to the eye from out-turned eyelids.

entropion damage to the eye from in-turned eyelids.

estrus when a female dog (bitch) is ready for mating (also called being in season, being in heat).

fallow pale cream to light fawn.

fault a characteristic that is not in keeping with breed standard.

feathering long hair fringing the ears, legs, tail and body.

foxy alert, keen expression; pointed, fox-like face.

gaze hound a hound that hunts by sight (also called a sighthound).

gestation period from conception to birth (usually about 60 days in dogs).

grizzle blue-gray color.

guard hairs stiff, long hairs that extend beyond the undercoat.

gundogs dogs bred to work with hunters in the field (also known as sporting dogs).

hackles hairs on neck and back that rise when dog is feeling fearful or aggressive.

harlequin white with blue or black patches.

haw membrane in inside corner of eye (third eyelid).

inbreeding the mating of closely related animals (also called linebreeding).

in heat see estrus.

in season see estrus.

liver chocolate or brown color.

mane long hair around the neck.

mask dark shading on face.

merle blue-gray with black flecks.

molting the seasonal loss of undercoat; shedding.

muzzle projecting part of head, including mouth, nose and jaws.

otter tail a thick, round tail, such as that of a Labrador, that tapers to the end from a thick base.

particolor an even mix of at least two colors.

prick ear erect, pointed ear.

quarry a hunting term for prey.

roan white mixed finely and evenly with another color.

ruff a collar of fur that is longer than the rest of the coat.

sable white with black shading.

saddle hair of contrasting color, length or texture in the shape of a saddle over the back.

salt and pepper mix of black and white hairs.

scenthound a hound that hunts and tracks by smell.

sighthound a hound that hunts by sight (also called a gaze hound).

slate dark gray color.

smooth coat short, flat-lying coat.

solid color uniform coat of one color.

Spitz a family of several breeds of powerful dogs from northern countries. They are characterized by their wedge-shaped heads, erect ears and thick double coats.

stacking placing a dog in the correct pose to show off its best features to a show judge.

stop indentation between the forehead and muzzle.

stripping removal of dead hairs from a dog's coat.

ticked black or dark tipped hairs in a light-colored coat.

topcoat strong, resistant outer coat.

topknot long hair on top of head, often tied up to protect the eyes.

topline the outline of the dog between the withers and the tail.

tricolor coat of three distinct colors.

undercoat dense, soft coat for insulation; sometimes water resistant.

wheaten pale yellow or fawn.

whelping giving birth to puppies.

whole color coat of one solid, unbroken color.

wirehaired harsh, dense coat.

withers a point just behind the neck, from which a dog's height is calculated.

INDEX

Page numbers in *italics* indicate illustrations and photos.

Acknowledgments

(t = top; b = bottom; c = center; l = left; r = right; Bg = background)

Photograph Credits

All photographs by Stuart Bowey/Ad-Libitum except:

Australian Picture Library 10–11c, 186c (Corbis). **Bruce Coleman Ltd** 86b (A. Bacchella). **Corbis Corp.** 1c, 13c, 18b, 41r, 83c, 115c. **Getty Images** 2c (FPG); 6–7c, 114–115c (Tony Stone Images). **Corel Corp.** 3c, 20Bg, 23t, 121b, 127t, 177t, 197c, 226c, 227c, 259c. **Norvia Behling** 287c. **PhotoDisc** 34–35c, 87t, 88–89c, 96b, 114Bg, 119t, 144Bg, 172Bg, 196Bg, 258Bg, 286Bg, 226Bg. **photolibrary.com** 8–9Bg (Bridgeman Art Library). **Tara Darling Paw Prints** 168c, 169t, 187t.

Illustration Credits

Virginia Gray 27, 57, 61, 110. **Janet Jones** 68, 69t, 72, 73, 74, 84, 85, 93, 106, 107, 108, 109, 110, 111. **Keith Scanlon** 69, 71, 75, 76. **Chris Wilson/Merilake** 52, 58, 70, 77, 102, 103, 104, 105.

The publishers would like to thank the following people for their assistance in the preparation of this book: Sarah Anderson, Kate Brady, Megan Wardle (editorial assistance); Jan Watson, Kelly Bourne (proofreading); Puddingburn Publishing Services (indexing).